Pocket
HONG KONG

TOP SIGHTS • LOCAL LIFE • MADE EASY

Piera Chen

In This Book

QuickStart Guide

Your keys to understanding the city – we help you decide what to do and how to do it

Need to Know
Tips for a smooth trip

Neighbourhoods
What's where

Explore Hong Kong

The best things to see and do, neighbourhood by neighbourhood

Top Sights
Make the most of your visit

Local Life
The insider's city

The Best of Hong Kong

The city's highlights in handy lists to help you plan

Best Walks
See the city on foot

Hong Kong' Best...
The best experiences

Survival Guide

Tips and tricks for a seamless, hassle-free city experience

Getting Around
Travel like a local

Essential Information
Including where to stay

Our selection of the city's best places to eat, drink and experience:

⊙ Sights

⊗ Eating

⊖ Drinking

✪ Entertainment

⊕ Shopping

These symbols give you the vital information for each listing:

🖍 Telephone Numbers		🖐 Family-Friendly	
⊙ Opening Hours		🐾 Pet-Friendly	
P Parking		🚌 Bus	
⊝ Nonsmoking		🚢 Ferry	
@ Internet Access		M Metro	
🕱 Wi-Fi Access		S Subway	
🖈 Vegetarian Selection		🚃 Tram	
🍴 English-Language Menu		🚆 Train	

Find each listing quickly on maps for each neighbourhood:

Bar Hemingway
16 ⊖ Map p233, B2

Legend has it that Hemi self, wielding a machine rate this timber-pan ered bar during showpiece is a en by Papa ar town. Dress s.com; Hôtel Rit ⊙6.30pm-2a

6 ⊙ Plac

Lonely Planet's Hong Kong

Lonely Planet Pocket Guides are designed to get you straight to the heart of the city.

Inside you'll find all the must-see sights, plus tips to make your visit to each one really memorable. We've split the city into easy-to-navigate neighbourhoods and provided clear maps so you'll find your way around with ease. Our expert authors have searched out the best of the city: walks, food, nightlife and shopping, to name a few. Because you want to explore, our 'Local Life' pages will take you to some of the most exciting areas to experience the real Hong Kong.

And of course you'll find all the practical tips you need for a smooth trip: itineraries for short visits; how to get around, and how much to tip the guy who serves you a drink at the end of a long day's exploration.

It's your guarantee of a really great experience.

Our Promise

You can trust our travel information because Lonely Planet authors visit the places we write about, each and every edition. We never accept freebies for positive coverage, so you can rely on us to tell it like it is.

The Best of Hong Kong 157

Hong Kong's Best Walks

Hong Kong's Best...

Survival Guide 183

QuickStart Guide

Welcome to Hong Kong

Like love, Hong Kong is an enigma. The city of glass towers, stellar kitchens and award-winning gangster Triad films is also home to crumbling villages, a Late Jurassic volcano and idyllic beaches teeming with fish and luxury yachts. It's a city full of pulse-quickening possibilities, yet solidly grounded by the rule of law and the world's best transport system.

Victoria Harbour
EDDYMTL/GETTY IMAGES ©

Hong Kong Top Sights

Star Ferry (p26)

At only $2, the 15-minute ride on the legendary Star Ferry, with its views of the urban coastline and Victoria Harbour, must be one of the world's best-value cruises.

Tsim Sha Tsui East Promenade (p96)

This promenade offers the best vantage points for viewing Hong Kong's most famous imagery: gleaming skyscrapers lined up between emerald hills and a deep-blue harbour.

Victoria Peak (p58)

Take Hong Kong's oldest thrill ride, the Peak Tram, for an almost-vertical climb up to the summit and Peak Tower for superlative views of the city and Victoria Harbour.

HSBC Building (p24)

Designed by Norman Foster, this feat of high-tech modernism in glass and steel houses the HSBC headquarters; it's one of Hong Kong's most iconic buildings.

Man Mo Temple (p28)

This important Taoist temple mesmerises with its unique history and a smoky air infused by incense coils dangling from the ceiling.

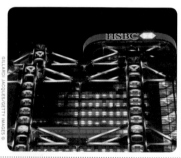

Temple Street Night Market (p114)

Beneath the glare of naked bulbs, stalls sell booty – from bric-a-brac to luggage. Nearby, fortune tellers beckon in English, and Cantonese opera singers strike a pose.

Happy Valley Racecourse (p64)

Whether you bet on the ponies or not, attending one of the Wednesday-evening meetings at this urban racecourse is one of the most exhilarating things to do in Hong Kong.

Sik Sik Yuen Wong Tai Sin Temple (p126)

The temple complex dedicated to a deified healer offers visual excitement, quirky landscaping, colourful Taoist ceremonies, and fortune telling (some in English).

Tian Tan Buddha (p138)

'Big Buddha' is the world's biggest seated outdoor bronze Buddha. He occupies a hilltop spot on leafy Lantau Island, but you can see him too as you fly into Hong Kong.

Ruins of the Church of St Paul (p144)

Macau's best-known landmark is this gorgeous facade, with fine carvings and detailed engravings, that was once part of a 17th-century Jesuit church.

Hong Kong Park (p62)

A top-notch aviary; photogenic lawns, ponds and waterfalls; and an exquisite tea-ware museum housed in a colonial building are the main draws of this manmade park.

Hong Kong Local Life

Insider tips to help you find the real city

Alongside Hong Kong's top sights, you can experience the city like a local by exploring the coolest hang-outs, the pet beaches, the favourite mountain trails, and those little indulgences that make up a Hong Konger's perfect day.

LKF & Soho Bar Crawl (p44)

▶ Amphitheatre
▶ Club 71

While it's not hard to have a good time anywhere in Lan Kwai Fong and Soho, there are some addresses favoured by local hipsters: some on account of the crowd they attract, some because of the quirky decor, and others because they could only exist in Hong Kong.

Wan Chai Breather (p66)

▶ Southorn Playground
▶ Rent-a-Curse Grannies

Life in the city can be stressful, and the older section of Wan Chai has a plethora of opportunities for people to regain their peace of mind. These run the gamut from gadget shopping and delicious food to folk sorcery and a cemetery.

Beach-Hopping on Island South (p86)

▶ Spices Restaurant
▶ South Bay

With beaches running from west to east, the southern coast of Hong Kong Island offers a seafront bazaar, restaurants with sea views, a balmy seaside promenade, kayaking and windsurfing opportunities, and of course, fine sands and clean water.

Hiking in the New Territories (p130)

▶ Tai Long Wan Trail
▶ Shing Mun Reservoir Trail

Hiking is so big in Hong Kong that at the first whiff of autumn, locals make a beeline for the hills. Here are a few easy-to-slightly-difficult trails featuring a range of vistas: volcanic formations and reservoir structures, verdant hills and balmy beaches, old miners' homes and butterflies, and an old Hakka village.

Lamma Island (p140)

▶ Main Street, Yung Shue Wan
▶ Lamcombe Seafood Restaurant

Laidback Lamma's soundtrack is reggae. You can

Market scene, Wan Chai

Repulse Bay (p87)

spend a great afternoon there soaking up the village vibes and feasting on seafood. For those with more time, opportunities abound for easy hiking, beach bumming, impromptu picnics, even learning about the island's fishing culture.

Exploring Taipa & Coloane Islands
(p146)

▶ Taipa House Museum
▶ Chapel of St Francis Xavier

With a handful of charming temples, an eccentric Catholic chapel, and traditional shops, Macau's islands of Taipa and Coloane have a lot to offer. If you want to play the tables, you can do that too.

CHRIS MELLOR/GETTY IMAGES ©

Other great places to experience the city like a local:

Wan Chai's Markets (p82)

Shanghai Street (p117)

Charming Tai Ping Shan Street (p35)

Macau's Sword Master (p150)

Delicious Century-Long Noodles (p38)

Getting Inked in Hong Kong (p123)

Learn Taichi for Free (p99)

Dance, Dance! (p55)

Chan Wah Kee Cutlery Store (p124)

Hankering for Pampering? (p39)

Hong Kong Day Planner

Day One

☀ Catch the Peak Tram up to **Victoria Peak** (p58) for stunning views of the city. Then descend and walk to **Sheung Wan** (p22), checking out the shopping options along the way. Stop at **Man Mo Temple** (p28) for a taste of history. Hungry? Saunter over to **Luk Yu Teahouse** (p49) for excellent dim sum.

☀ Take the **Star Ferry** (p26) to Kowloon. Enjoy the views along **Tsim Sha Tsui East Promenade** (p96) as you stroll to the **Hong Kong Museum of History** (p99) for some context to your day's impressions.

☾ After an early dinner at **Yin Yang** (p73) in Wan Chai, take the tram to **Lan Kwai Fong and Soho** for drinks (p44).

Day Two

☀ Visit the lovely **Hong Kong Park** (p62), then head over to Queen's Rd East to explore the temples and old streets of **Wan Chai** (p70). Tram it to Causeway Bay for gift-shopping at **G.O.D.** (p81). Have lunch at **Old Bazaar Kitchen** (p75) and take the MTR to Tsim Sha Tsui.

☀ Visit the **Former Marine Police Headquarters** (p100), then amble down Nathan Rd to the **Former Kowloon British School** (p100) and **St Andrew's Church** (p99). Have afternoon tea at the **Peninsula Hotel** (p101), then do some shopping in Tsim Sha Tsui (p109).

☾ Dine at one of the street stalls at **Temple Street Night Market** (p114). If you want to go on, have a drink at **Fullcup Café** (p122), then in the wee hours of the morning make your way to Yau Ma Tei **Wholesale Fruit Market** (p118) to see stall owners negotiating prices and workmen delivering truckloads of fresh fruit.

Short on time?
We've arranged Hong Kong's must-sees into these day-by-day itineraries to make sure you see the very best of the city in the time you have available.

Day Three

 Take the bus to Aberdeen for a sampan cruise of the **Aberdeen Typhoon Shelter** (p89), then head over to **Ap Lei Chau Market Cooked Food Centre** (p90) to check out the indoor wet market in the old town. Have lunch at any one of the small eateries in the old town. Follow with shopping (for bargain furniture and clothing) at **Horizon Plaza** (p93).

Spend the rest of the afternoon and early evening admiring temples: Taoist **Sik Sik Yuen Wong Tai Sin Temple** (p126) and Buddhist **Chi Lin Nunnery** (p127). Have dinner there too, at Chi Lin Vegetarian.

After dinner, head to Causeway Bay for fine Japanese whisky and fancy mixology action at **b.a.r. Executive Bar** (p77). Head back to Tsim Sha Tsui for drinks at **Ned Kelly's Last Stand** (p107).

Day Four

 Start your third day with a free **taichi class** (p108) compliments of the Hong Kong Tourism Board. Then bus it to Yau Ma Tei to check out **Tin Hau Temple** (p117), the **Jade Market** (p117) and the traditional shops on **Shanghai Street** (p117). Take the MTR to Central, and have lunch at **Sushi Kuu** (p50).

Shop for gifts at **Shanghai Tang** (p40) in Central and **G.O.D.** (p81) in Causeway Bay. If it's gadgets you're after, make for **Wan Chai Computer Centre** (p82). Averse to shopping? If you haven't already, take the MTR to Wong Tai Sin in Kowloon to visit **Sik Sik Yuen Wong Tai Sin Temple** (p126).

 Have dinner at **Ye Shanghai** (p105) in Tsim Sha Tsui, then head to **Wan Chai's bars** (p76) for a final night of debauchery.

Need to Know

For more information, see Survival Guide (p183).

Currency
Hong Kong dollar ($) for Hong Kong, pataca (MOP$) for Macau.

Language
Cantonese, English and Mandarin. Also Portuguese for Macau.

Visas
Not required for visitors from the US, Australia, New Zealand, Canada, the EU, Israel and South Africa for up to 30 days.

Money
ATMs widely available. Credit cards accepted in most hotels and restaurants; some budget places only take cash.

Mobile Phones
Set your phone to roaming, or buy a local SIM card if you need to make lots of calls.

Time
Hong Kong Time (GMT/UTC plus eight hours)

Plugs & Adaptors
Plugs are UK-style with three square prongs. North American visitors will need an adaptor and/or transformer. Most convenience stores sell adaptors.

Tipping
Taxi drivers only expect you to round up to the nearest dollar. Many restaurants add a 10% service charge to the bill.

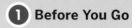 **Before You Go**

Your Daily Budget

Budget less than $600
► Guesthouse $130 to $350

► Food at a *cha chaan tang* (teahouse) or *dai pai dong* (hawker-style food stall) $50 to $90

Midrange $600 to $1600
► Hotel room $520 to $880

► Dinner at midrange Chinese restaurant from $300 per person

Top End more than $1600
► Boutique or four-star hotel room $2000

► Dinner at top Chinese restaurant from $800 per person

Useful Websites

Lonely Planet (www.lonelyplanet.com /hong-kong) Destination information, hotel bookings, traveller information and more.

Discover Hong Kong (www.discover hongkong.com) Solid tourist-authority website.

Urbtix (www.urbtix.hk) Book tickets to entertainment events in town.

Time Out Hong Kong (www.timeout.com .hk) Events and entertainment listings.

Advance Planning

Two months before Check dates of Chinese festivals; book tickets for major performances; book a table at top restaurants.

One month Book tickets for fringe festivals, live shows; book a table at popular restaurants.

Two weeks Book harbour cruises, nature tours.

One week Check the weather.

② Arriving in Hong Kong

Fly into Hong Kong International Airport (HKIA; www.hongkongairport.com), or cross the border at Lo Wu or Lok Ma Chau from Shenzhen on mainland China by bus or train (www.mtr.com.hk). Transport to the city centre is easy and convenient.

✈ Hong Kong International Airport

Destination	Best Transport
Central	Airport Express; Air Bus A11
Sheung Wan, Wan Chai & Causeway Bay	Airport Express then taxi; Air Bus A11
Aberdeen & South	Air Bus A10
Tsim Sha Tsui, Yau Ma Tei & Mong Kok	Airport Express then taxi; Air Bus A21

Lo Wu & Lok Ma Chau border gates

Destination	Best Transport
Admiralty, Central & Tsim Sha Tsui	MTR East Line to Kwun Tong Line to Tsuen Wan Line
Sheung Wan, Wan Chai & Causeway Bay	MTR as per Central, change at Central to Island Line.
Yau Ma Tei & Mong Kok	MTR East Line to Kwun Tong Line

At the Airport

At Hong Kong International Airport, two **Customer Services Centres** (arrivals hall ⊘7am-11pm, departures hall ⊘5am-1am) provide maps; money-exchange and banking counters; ATMs; duty-free shops; and pay or courtesy phones. A couple of counters at the arrivals hall help with accommodation or car hire. A short-term baggage storage facility is located on Level 3 of Terminal 2.

③ Getting Around

Hong Kong's efficient Mass Transit Railway (MTR) system, comprehensive bus network, and ferries to outlying islands will take you almost anywhere you need to go. A prepaid Octopus card can be used on most forms of public transport in Hong Kong. For shorter stays, buy a one-day or three-day pass for unlimited rides on the MTR. They are available at any MTR station.

Ⓜ MTR

Hong Kong's subway and train system covers most of the city and is the easiest way to get around; most lines run from 6am to midnight.

🚌 Bus

Extensive network and ideal for short rides; most lines run from 6am to midnight.

🚃 Tram

Runs on the northern strip of Hong Kong Island. Slow but great views; runs from 6am to midnight.

⛴ Ferry

Star Ferry connects Hong Kong Island and Kowloon through the scenic harbour; runs from 6.30am to 11.30pm. More modern ferry fleets run between Central and outlying islands.

Hong Kong Neighbourhoods

Temple Street Night Market

Hong Kong Island: Lan Kwai Fong & Soho (p42)
Art galleries, stylish bars and life – surprisingly simple and unadorned – grace the streets of Hong Kong's partying epicentre.

Hong Kong Island: Central & Sheung Wan (p22)
Central: high finance meets haute couture; Sheung Wan: temples, antiques and fine art.

⊙ Top Sights
HSBC Building

Star Ferry

Man Mo Temple

Hong Kong Island: Aberdeen & the South (p84)
Sunny beaches, a balmy bazaar, white-knuckle mechanical rides, sampan cruises and yummy seafood.

Star Ferry

Man Mo Temple

HSBC Building

Victoria Peak

Hong Kong Park

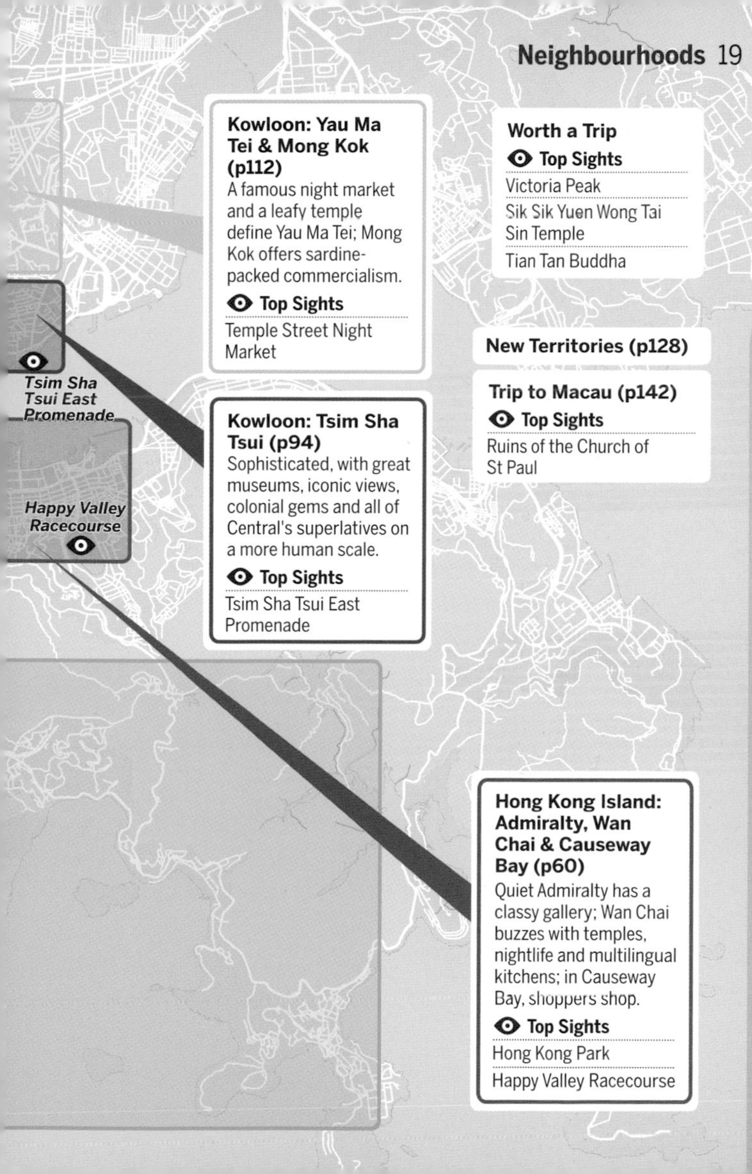

Kowloon: Yau Ma Tei & Mong Kok (p112)

A famous night market and a leafy temple define Yau Ma Tei; Mong Kok offers sardine-packed commercialism.

◉ Top Sights

Temple Street Night Market

Worth a Trip

◉ Top Sights

Victoria Peak

Sik Sik Yuen Wong Tai Sin Temple

Tian Tan Buddha

New Territories (p128)

Trip to Macau (p142)

◉ Top Sights

Ruins of the Church of St Paul

Kowloon: Tsim Sha Tsui (p94)

Sophisticated, with great museums, iconic views, colonial gems and all of Central's superlatives on a more human scale.

◉ Top Sights

Tsim Sha Tsui East Promenade

◉
Tsim Sha Tsui East Promenade

Happy Valley Racecourse
◉

Hong Kong Island: Admiralty, Wan Chai & Causeway Bay (p60)

Quiet Admiralty has a classy gallery; Wan Chai buzzes with temples, nightlife and multilingual kitchens; in Causeway Bay, shoppers shop.

◉ Top Sights

Hong Kong Park

Happy Valley Racecourse

Explore
Hong Kong

Worth a Trip

Causeway Bay
MICHAEL COYNE/GETTY IMAGES ©

Explore

Hong Kong Island: Central & Sheung Wan

The business heart of Hong Kong, sharp-suited Central is a heady mix of exclusive boutiques, peaceful parks, fine dining, corporate cathedrals and a few historic buildings (including a real cathedral). Arguably even more rewarding to explore, Sheung Wan carries the echo of 'Old Hong Kong' in places, with its traditional shops, temples and steep 'ladder streets', which are composed entirely of stairs.

The Sights in a Day

☀ If it's a weekday, avoid taking the MTR during the morning rush hour (7.30am to 9am). Alternatively, arrive by Star Ferry. Spend an hour or two visiting **Man Mo Temple** (pictured left; p28) and temples nearby, when elders come to light their morning incense. Explore the neighbourhood, surrendering to the smells of wet markets and dried seafood shops. Beat the noon-to-2pm crowds by having an early bite at **The Chairman** (p36).

☀ View the latest exhibition at the well-curated **Para/Site Art Space** (p35) and shop for funky trinkets at **Cat Street Bazaar** (p35). Over the next couple of hours, check out the architecture in the vicinity – glass-and-steel modernity like the **HSBC Building** (p24) and colonial-era survivors like **St John's Cathedral** (p33). Then either relax at the **Zoological & Botanical Gardens** (p33) or take afternoon tea at **Sevva** (p39). Recharged, make a beeline for the boutiques of **IFC Mall** (p41).

☾ Have dinner at **Lung King Heen** (p37) or **Linguini Fini** (p38). Spend the rest of the night sipping cocktails at **Sevva** (p39).

👁 Top Sights

HSBC Building (p24)

Star Ferry (p26)

Man Mo Temple (p28)

♥ Best of Hong Kong

Eating

Lung King Heen (p37)

Tim's Kitchen (p36)

The Chairman (p36)

Views

Bank of China Tower (p32)

Caprice (p38)

Star Ferry (p26)

Getting There

Ⓜ **MTR** Central station (Island and Tsuen Wan lines); Hong Kong station (Airport Express); Sheung Wan station (Island line).

🚌 **Bus** Island buses stop at Central bus terminus below Exchange Sq; bus 26 links Central with Sheung Wan.

🚋 **Tram** Along Des Voeux Rd Central and Des Voeux Rd West.

⛴ **Star Ferry** From Tsim Sha Tsui to Central Pier 7.

Top Sights
HSBC Building

The stunning HSBC headquarters, designed by British architect Norman Foster in 1985, is a masterpiece of precision, sophistication and innovation. And so it should be. On completion it was the world's most expensive building (costing more than US$1 billion). The 52-storey building reflects the architect's wish to create areas of public and private space, and to break the mould of previous bank architecture. A lighting scheme fitted later enabled the building to maintain its splendour at night.

◉ Map p30, G4

滙豐總行大廈

www.hsbc.com.hk/1/2/about/home/unique-headquarters

1 Queen's Rd

admission free

⊙ escalator 9am-4.30pm Mon-Fri, to 12.30pm Sat

Ⓜ Central, exit K

Don't Miss

Stephen & Stitt

The two bronze lions guarding the main entrance were designed for the bank's previous headquarters in 1935. The lions are known as Stephen – the one roaring – and Stitt, after two bank employees of the time. The Japanese used the lions as target practice during the occupation; you can still see bullet holes on Stitt. Rub their mighty paws for luck.

Feng Shui

Examples of good feng shui abound. The building has unobstructed views of Victoria Harbour – water is associated with prosperity. The escalators are meant to symbolise the whiskers of a dragon sucking wealth into its belly. And they're built at an angle to the entrance to disorient evil spirits, which can only travel in a straight line.

Lighting

The 52-storey glass-and-aluminum building was installed with around 700 lighting units, including colour-changing fluorescent lights, 18 years after it was built. The project, costing $5.5 million, ensured the building dazzled as much at night as it did in broad daylight.

Atrium

The atrium located on the 3rd floor has greenery cascading from the different floors and is flooded with natural light. There's no prettier setting in which to get your money changed.

☑ Top Tips

▶ The ground floor is public space; you can traverse and use its ATMs without entering the bank.

▶ Take the escalator to the 3rd floor to gaze at the cathedral-like atrium.

▶ If you want to use banking services without having to queue, avoid office lunch hours.

▶ The HSBC Building isn't Central's only iconic skyscraper; if you're an architecture buff, also check out the Bank of China Tower (p32) and Two IFC (p32).

✗ Take a Break

For million-dollar views of the HSBC Building and/or other stunners, head to the terrace of stylish restaurant and bar **Sevva** (p39) or the al fresco area of **Red Bar** (Map p30, F2; ✆ 8129 8882; www.pure-red.com; level 4, Two IFC; ◷ noon-midnight Mon-Thu, noon-3am Fri & Sat, noon-10pm Sun).

Top Sights
Star Ferry

No trip to Hong Kong is complete without a ride on the Star Ferry, that fleet of electric-diesel vessels with names like *Morning Star* and *Twinkling Star*. At any time of the day the ride, with its riveting views of skyscrapers and mountains, must be one of the world's best-value cruises. At the end of the 10-minute journey, watch as a hemp rope is cast and caught with a billhook, just as it was in 1888 when the first boat docked.

◉ Map p30, G1

天星小輪

www.starferry.com.hk

adult $2-3, child $1.40-1.80

🕓 Central–Tsim Sha Tsui every 6-12 minutes 6.30am-11.30pm, Wan Chai–Tsim Sha Tsui, every 8-20 minutes, 7.20am-11pm

Don't Miss

Kowloon Concourse

In 1910 the Kowloon–Canton Railway was built near the Kowloon concourse, linking Hong Kong with the mainland. On Christmas Day 1941 the colonial governor took the ferry to Tsim Sha Tsui, where he surrendered to the Japanese at the Peninsula Hotel. You can still see the Clock Tower of the original train station and, of course, the Peninsula Hotel. In 1966 thousands gathered at the Kowloon concourse to protest against a fare increase. The protest erupted into the 1966 Riot, the first in a series of important social protests leading to colonial reform.

Piers

The pier on Hong Kong Island is an uninspiring Edwardian replica that was built to replace the old pier at Edinburgh Pl – in streamline moderne style and with a clock tower – that was demolished despite vehement opposition from Hong Kong people. The Kowloon pier, resembling a finger pointing at the Island, remains untouched.

The Logo

The Star Ferry was founded in 1880 by a Parsee from Bombay who was living in Hong Kong. Parsees are Zoroastrian, a religion from Persia, and the five-pointed star on the Star Ferry logo is in fact an ancient Zoroastrian symbol. In the Christmas tale, the three magi from the East who followed the star to Bethlehem, were Zoroastrian pilgrims.

☑ Top Tips

▶ Take your first trip on a clear night from Kowloon to Central. It's more dramatic in this direction.

▶ For a surreal experience, take a ride during the nightly Symphony of Lights laser show (between 8pm and 8.20pm).

▶ If you don't mind noise and fumes, the lower deck (only open on the Tsim Sha Tsui–Central route) is better for photos.

▶ The coin-operated turnstiles take exact change or the Octopus card; you can get change from the ticket window.

✕ Take a Break

For a beer and a bite, ascend to **Pier 7** (Map p30, G1; www.cafedecogroup .com; ⊙9am-midnight, happy hr 6-9pm) on the rooftop viewing deck of the Star Ferry Pier. Or buy snacks and drinks from the shops near Central Piers and consume while people-watching.

Top Sights
Man Mo Temple

One of Hong Kong's oldest temples and a declared monument, atmospheric Man Mo Temple is dedicated to the gods of literature ('Man') and of war ('Mo'). Built in 1847 during the Qing dynasty by wealthy Chinese merchants, it was, besides a place of worship, a court of arbitration for local disputes in the 19th century when trust was thin between the local Chinese and the colonialists. Oaths taken at this Taoist temple (accompanied by the ritual beheading of a rooster) were accepted by the colonial government.

👁 Map p30, C2

文武廟

☎ 2540 0350

124-126 Hollywood Rd

admission free

🕙 8am-6pm

🚌 26

Don't Miss

Outside the Entrance

Here are four gilt plaques on poles that used to be carried at processions. Two describe the gods being worshipped inside, one requests silence and a show of respect within the temple's grounds, and the last warns women who are menstruating to keep out of the main hall as the blood is believed to put them in a state of ritual defilement.

Main Hall

Two gold-plated sedan chairs with elaborate carvings sit here. They used to carry the statues of the deities during festivals. Lending the temple its beguiling and smoky air are rows of large earth-coloured spirals suspended from the roof, like strange fungi in an upside-down garden. These are incense coils burned as offerings by worshippers.

Lit Shing Kung

Off to the side of the main hall is 'saints' palace', built around the same time as the temple. It's a place of worship for other Buddhist and Taoist deities, including the goddess of mercy and Tai Sui, the 60 heavenly generals who each represent a particular year in the 60-year cycle of the Chinese almanac.

Kung Sor

This hall, with its name literally meaning 'public meeting place', used to serve as a court of justice to settle disputes in the Chinese community before the modern judicial system was introduced. A couplet at the entrance urges those entering to leave their selfish interests and prejudices outside.

☑ Top Tips

▶ The English-speaking fortune teller, Master Ng (11.30am to 4.30pm, random days off) charges $500 to tell your fortune and $20 to interpret a fortune stick.

▶ You'll see a canister filled with fortune sticks in the temple. You can shake the canister, tilting it slightly, until a stick falls out. Each stick has a number corresponding to lines of text, which the fortune teller can interpret for you.

✕ Take a Break

Coffee and gourmet sandwiches await at **Java Java** (Map p30, B2; http://javajavalounge.com; 188 Hollywood Rd; ◷8am-9pm Mon-Thu, to midnight Fri & Sat, 9am-9pm Sun). Heading east? Munch on pastas and salads at **Classified the Cheese Room** (Map p30, C2; www.classifiedfoodshops.com.hk; 108 Hollywood Rd, Sheung Wan; meals $150-300; ◷noon-11pm Mon-Fri, 10am-11pm Sat & Sun).

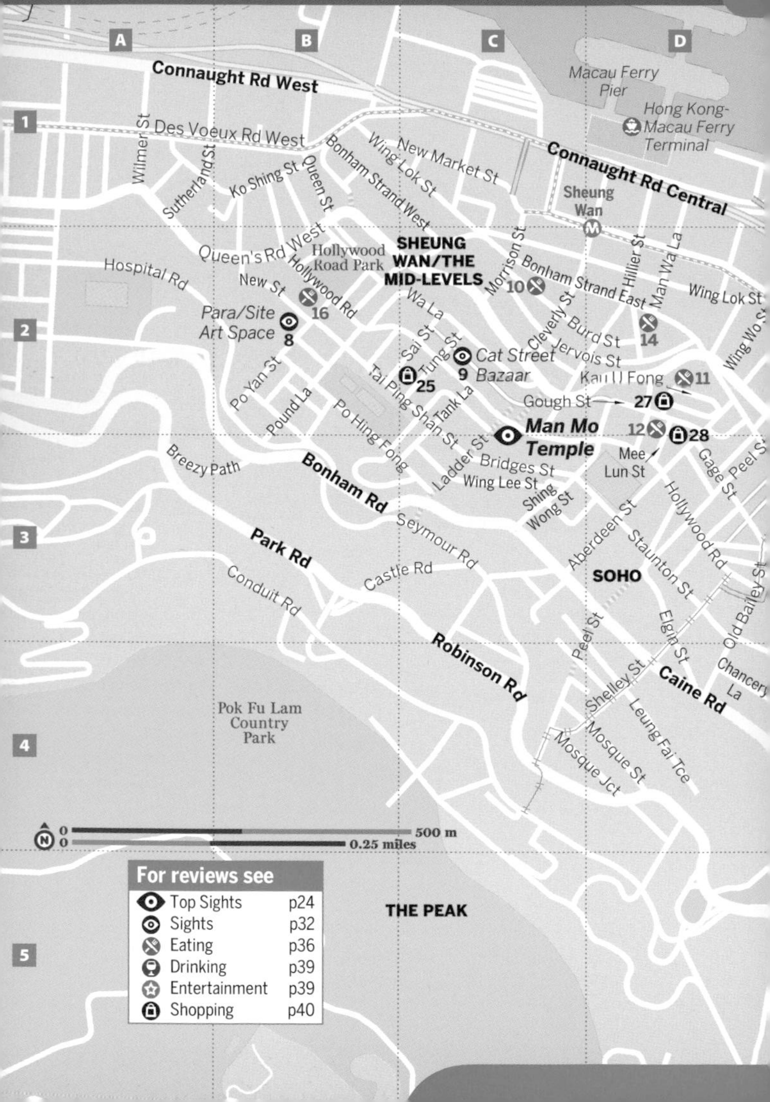

Connaught Rd West

A   B   C   D

Des Voeux Rd West

Wilmer St

Macau Ferry Pier

Hong Kong–Macau Ferry Terminal

Connaught Rd Central

1

Ko Shing St

Queen St

Wing Lok St

New Market St

Bonham Strand West

Sutherland St

Sheung Wan

Hospital Rd

Queen's Rd West

Hollywood Rd

Hollywood Road Park

SHEUNG WAN/THE MID-LEVELS

Bonham Strand East

Morrison St

Hillier St

Man Wa La

New St

10 ⊗

Wing Lok St

Wing Wo St

2

Para/Site Art Space

8 ⊙

16 ⊙

Wa La

Cleverly St

Burd St

Jervois St

14 ⊗

Po Yan St

25 🔒

Ta La

Ko Tung St

Cat Street

Bazaar

9 ⊙

Kau U Fong

11 ⊗

Pound La

Tai Ping Shan St

Tank La

Gough St

27 🔒

Man Mo Temple

12 ⊗

28 🔒

Breezy Path

Po Hing Fong

Ladder St

Bridges St

Wing Lee St

Mee Lun St

Bonham Rd

3

Park Rd

Seymour Rd

Shing Wong St

Aberdeen St

Staunton St

Hollywood Rd

Gage St

Peel St

SOHO

Old Bailey St

Conduit Rd

Castle Rd

Peel St

Elgin St

Chancery La

Robinson Rd

Shelley St

Leung Fai Tce

Caine Rd

4

Pok Fu Lam Country Park

Mosque St

Mosque Jct

⊲N 0   500 m
  0   0.25 miles

5

THE PEAK

For reviews see	
⊙ Top Sights	p24
⊙ Sights	p32
⊗ Eating	p36
🍷 Drinking	p39
★ Entertainment	p39
🔒 Shopping	p40

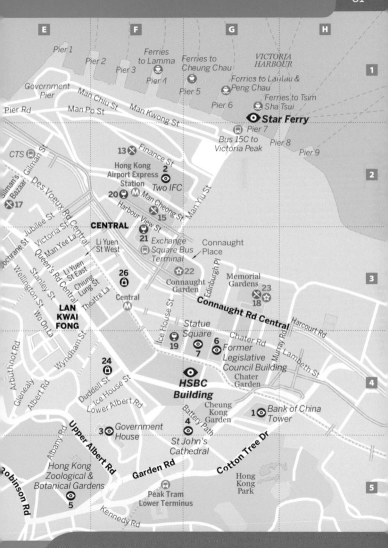

E

Pier 1
Pier 2

F

Ferries to Lamma
Pier 3
Ferries to Cheung Chau
Pier 4

G

VICTORIA HARBOUR

H

Ferries to Lantau & Peng Chau
Pier 5
Pier 6
Ferries to Tsim Sha Tsui

Government Pier
Man Chiu St
Man Kwong St
Man Po St
Pier Rd

◉ Star Ferry
Pier 7
Bus 15C to Victoria Peak
Pier 8
Pier 9

CTS 🚇
Gilman's Bazaar
Gilman St
Des Voeux Rd Central
Jubilee St
🚇 17

13 ✕ Finance St
Hong Kong Airport Express Station
2 ◉
Two IFC
20 🚇 Ⓜ Man Cheong St
Harbour View St
15
CENTRAL
21 🚇
Exchange Square Bus Terminal
Connaught Place

Man Yu St

Victoria St
Cochrane St
Queen's Rd Central
Man Yee La
Li Yuen St West
Li Yuen St East
Chiung Lung St
Theatre La
Stanley St
Wellington St
Wo On La

26 🔒
Central Ⓜ

Li Yuen St West

🏛 22
Connaught Garden

Memorial Gardens
✕ 23
18 🏛

Connaught Rd Central

Ice House St

Statue Square
19 ◉
6 ◉
7 ◉

Chater Rd
Former Legislative Council Building
Chater Garden

Harcourt Rd
Murray Rd
Lambeth St

LAN KWAI FONG
Wyndham St

24 🔒

Arbuthnot Rd
Glenealy
Albert Rd

Duddell St
Ice House St
Lower Albert Rd

◉
HSBC Building

Cheung Kong Garden
Battery Path

1 ◉ Bank of China Tower

3 ◉ Government House

4 ◉
St John's Cathedral

Upper Albert Rd

Albany Rd

Hong Kong Zoological & Botanical Gardens
5 ◉

Robinson Rd

Garden Rd

🚋
Peak Tram Lower Terminus

Kennedy Rd

Cotton Tree Dr

Hong Kong Park

1

2

3

4

5

Sights

Bank of China Tower BUILDING

 Map p30, G4

Designed by IM Pei, Hong Kong's third-tallest building has an asymmetrical form comprising cubes and prisms. Some locals say its jagged silhouette evokes a meat cleaver poised to chop the HSBC Building. The observation deck (42nd floor) has views extending to Kowloon (中銀大廈; www.bochk.com; 1 Garden Rd; ◷8am-6pm Mon-Fri; ⓜCentral, exit K)

Two IFC BUILDING

 Map p30, F2

This 88-storey colossus is Hong Kong's second-tallest building. Designed partly by Cesar Pelli, it's been christened Sir YK Pao's Erection, a reference to the developer who built it. The Hong Kong Monetary Authority Information Centre (金管局資訊中心), on the 55th floor, runs guided tours (◷2.30pm Mon-Fri, 10.30am Sat). (國際金融中心二期; www.info.gov.hk/hkma; 8 Finance St; ⓜHong Kong, exit E1)

Government House BUILDING

 Map p30, F4

Parts of this erstwhile official residence of the top man in Hong Kong date back to 1855. Other features were added by the Japanese, who used it as military headquarters during the occupation of Hong Kong in WWII. It's open to the public three or four times a year, notably one Sunday in March, when the azaleas are in full bloom.

Understand
Walls in Sheung Wan

In the 19th century many Chinese flocked to Hong Kong from the mainland in search of employment. The majority were coolies who settled in Sheung Wan. Afraid they'd get too close to the Europeans living nearby, the British imposed a segregation policy: Chinese to the west, Europeans to the east, with Aberdeen St serving as the invisible wall between the two. Conditions in the Chinese quarter were atrocious. The British turned a blind eye, and a bubonic plague broke out in 1894, killing 20,000.

From the time of the plague until after WWII, other walls were erected in Sheung Wan. To prevent landslides on steep Hong Kong Island, masonry workers shored up many slopes adjacent to main roads with stone retaining walls. Open joints between the stones allowed strong species such as Chinese banyans to sprout, further strengthening the walls.

Today Sheung Wan is one of Hong Kong's most cosmopolitan areas, but the 'wall trees' are still there.

BLOOMBERG/GETTY IMAGES ©

City skyline including Two IFC

(香港禮賓府; ☎2530 2003; www.ceo.gov
.hk/gh; Upper Albert Rd, Central; admission
free; 🚌3B, 12)

St John's Cathedral CHURCH

4 👁 Map p30, G4

This Anglican cathedral, built in the
shape of a cross, is a relic of Hong
Kong's colonial past. It suffered heavy
damage during WWII; after the war
the front doors were remade using
timber salvaged from the British war-
ship HMS *Tamar,* and the beautiful
stained glass was replaced. Enter from
Battery Path. (聖約翰座堂; ☎2523 4157;
www.stjohnscathedral.org.hk; 4-8 Garden Rd,
Central; ⊙7am-6pm; Ⓜ Central, exit J2)

Hong Kong Zoological & Botanical Gardens GARDENS

5 👁 Map p30, E5

These 5.6-hectare gardens, which first
welcomed visitors in 1864, are a pleasant assembly of fountains, sculptures,
greenhouses, a zoo and some fabulous
aviaries. There are hundreds of species
of birds in residence, as well as exotic
trees, plants and shrubs. (香港動植物
公園; www.lcsd.gov.hk/parks/hkzbg; Albany
Rd, Central; ⊙terrace gardens 6am-10pm,
zoo & aviaries 6am-7pm, greenhouses 9am-
4.30pm; 🚌3B, 12)

Understand

British Colonisation & Its End

Until European traders imported opium into Hong Kong, it was an obscure backwater in the Chinese empire. The British developed the trade aggressively and by the start of the 19th century were trading this 'foreign mud' for Chinese tea, silk and porcelain.

Opium Wars

China's attempts to end the opium trade gave Britain a pretext for military action; gunboats were sent in. In 1841 the Union Jack was hoisted on Hong Kong Island, and the Treaty of Nanking, which ended the so-called First Opium War, ceded the island to the British crown 'in perpetuity'.

At the end of the Second Opium War in 1860, Britain took possession of Kowloon Peninsula and, in 1898, a 99-year lease was granted for the New Territories.

Transformation

Through the 20th century Hong Kong grew in fits and starts. Waves of refugees fled China for Hong Kong. Trade flourished, as did British expat social life, until Japan crashed the party in 1941.

By the end of WWII Hong Kong's population had plummeted. But trouble in China again saw refugees push the population beyond 2 million. This, together with a UN trade embargo on China during the Korean War and China's isolation, enabled Hong Kong to reinvent itself as one of the world's most dynamic ports and manufacturing and financial-service centres.

Return of Sovereignty

In 1984 Britain agreed to return Hong Kong to China in 1997, on the condition it would retain its free-market economy and its social and legal systems for 50 years. On 1 July 1997 the British era ended.

In March 2012 Leung Chun-ying became Hong Kong's fourth chief executive. Though seemingly more decisive than his predecessors, Leung's unsubstantiated 'red' connections have worried many Hong Kongers, something not helped by the city's spiralling living costs.

Former Legislative Council Building
HISTORIC BUILDING

6 Map p30, G4

This colonnaded, domed neoclassical building is the former Supreme Court, built in 1912 of granite quarried on Stonecutter Island. Standing atop the pediment is a blindfolded statue of Themis, the Greek goddess of justice. (立法會大樓; 8 Jackson Rd, Central; Ⓜ Central, exit J1)

Statue Square
SQUARE

7 Map p30, G4

This leisurely square, which used to house effigies of British royalty, now pays tribute to a single sovereign – the founder of HSBC. In the square's northern part is the 1923 **cenotaph** (和平紀念碑), a memorial to Hong Kong residents killed during the two world wars. To the east is the **Hong Kong Club Building** (香港會所大廈; 1 Jackson Rd), a gentlemen's club designed by Australian Harry Siedler, with opposing curves reminiscent of a swimming stingray. On the south side of Chater Rd, Statue Sq is a pleasant collection of fountains and seating areas. (皇后像廣場; Edinburgh Pl, Central; Ⓜ Central, exit K)

Para/Site Art Space
GALLERY

8 Map p30, B2

This small but adventurous, nonprofit art space knows no boundaries when it comes to mixing media. Most exhibitions have a local focus, but some also feature international artists.

Charming Tai Ping Shan Street

Tai Ping Shan St, the hub of the old Chinese quarter back when there was racial segregation, has a chill neighbourhood vibe and quaint cafes. But it's best known for its three old **temples** (太平山街廟宇; Map p30, B2; 42, 34 & 9 Tai Ping Shan St; ⏱8am-6pm; 🚌26). **Pak Sing Ancestral Hall** (百姓廟, c 1851), the 'people's temple', was a clinic for Chinese patients refusing treatment by Western medicine, and a store-room for bodies awaiting burial in China. **Kwun Yum Temple** (觀音堂) worships the goddess of mercy. You can ID your Chinese zodiac animal and burn incense for it at **Tai Sui Temple** (太歲廟).

Para/Site is located at the western end of Hollywood Rd. (藝術空間; ☎2517 4620; www.para-site.org.hk; 4 Po Yan St, Sheung Wan; admission free; ⏱noon-7pm Wed-Sun; Ⓜ Sheung Wan, 🚌26)

Cat Street Bazaar
MARKET

9 Map p30, C2

Officially named Upper Lascar Row, 'Cat St' is a mini flea market of antiques and curios. There are authentic items, but most of what you see are fakes or rejects from some family's house move. That said, it's an interesting place to browse for gifts and souvenirs. Remember to bargain. (摩羅上街; ⏱9am-6pm; 🚌26)

Eating

Tim's Kitchen

CANTONESE **$$**

10 Map p30, C2

One of Hong Kong's top eateries according to gourmands, this understated place serves masterfully executed Cantonese fare and dim sum. Signature dishes such as crab claw poached with wintermelon require preordering. Reservations essential. (桃花源; ☎2581 9098; www .timskitchen.com.hk; 84-90 Bonham Strand, Sheung Wan; meals from $400; ⊙lunch & dinner Mon-Sat; Ⓜ Sheung Wan, exit A2)

The Chairman

CANTONESE **$$$**

11 Map p30, D2

Subtle faux-retro decor and warm service impart a homely feel at this upmarket place serving Cantonese classics with a modern twist. The majority of the dishes hit the right notes, from flavour to presentation. No surprise, given how serious the Chairman is about food – it even has a manifesto on its website. Reservations essential. (大班樓; ☎2555 2202; www.thechairmangroup.com; ground fl, 18 Kau U Fong, Sheung Wan; lunch/dinner from $178/528; ⊙lunch & dinner; Ⓜ Sheung Wan, exit E2)

IAN TROWER/JAI/CORBIS ©

City Hall Maxim's Palace (p38)

On Lot 10 FRENCH $$

12 ✗ Map p30, D2

At On Lot 10, rustic French dishes are prepared with skill and passion by chef-owner David Lai, who helmed the Alain Ducasse restaurants in Monaco and Hong Kong. The menu changes regularly but has included truffled salt-baked bresse chicken, roasted Pyrenees lamb, and sweetbreads cooked in more ways than you can dream of. (☎2155 9210; 34 Gough St, Sheung Wan; ☉lunch & dinner Mon-Sat; Ⓜ Sheung Wan, exit E2)

Lung King Heen CANTONESE, DIM SUM $$$

13 ✗ Map p30, F2

The world's first Chinese restaurant to receive three Michelin stars. The Cantonese food is excellently prepared and presented and, when combined with the harbour views and pristine service, makes for a truly unbeatable dining experience. The signature steamed lobster and scallop dumplings sell out early. (龍景軒; ☎3196 8888; www.four seasons.com/hongkong; Four Seasons Hotel, 8 Finance St; set lunch $400, set dinner $880; ☉noon-2.30pm Mon-Sat, 11.30am-3pm Sun, 6-10.30pm Mon-Sun; Ⓜ Hong Kong, exit E1)

Doppio Zero Trattoria ITALIAN $$

14 ✗ Map p30, D2

This cosy trattoria is a favourite with local foodies, some of whom visit almost every week for the whipped lardo, truffled fried oysters and handmade

Top Tip

Fine Dining the Cheap Way

To enjoy Central's gourmet European restaurants without breaking the bank, go for the lunch special menus – most restaurants have them for the convenience of business lunchers. Some high-end places may even serve breakfast and/or afternoon tea, or sell gourmet sandwiches at a takeaway station. Remember to book in advance if you're dining in for lunch.

pastas that include a tantalising beet-root ravioli. If you like beef, the grilled US rib-eye served with bone marrow is excellent value at $385. (☎2851 0682; www.doppiozero.com.hk; basement, The Pemberton, 22 Bonham Strand, Sheung Wan; meals from $300; ☉lunch & dinner Mon-Sat, 11am-4pm Sun; Ⓜ Sheung Wan, exit A2)

Tasty Congee & Noodle Wonton Shop NOODLES $

15 ✗ Map p30, F2

One of the more affordable places to dine in this luxury mall, this restaurant has a long line at lunch. So learn from the ladies of leisure – shop first, eat later. It'll be worth the wait – the hallmark shrimp wontons are so good even the loudish decor won't distract you. (正斗粥麵專家; www.tasty.com.hk; shop 3016-3018, IFC Mall, 1 Harbour View St; meals $75-100; ☉11.30am-10.45pm; Ⓜ Hong Kong, exit E1)

Local Life

Delicious Century-Long Noodles

Nothing warms the soul like a bowl of hearty beef brisket (牛腩, *ngau laam*) noodles from famous **Kau Kee** (九記; Map p30, D2; ☏2850 5967; 21 Gough St; meals from $40; ⏱12.30-7.15pm & 8.30-11.30pm Mon-Sat; Ⓜ Sheung Wan, exit E2). And the locals clearly know it – during the 90-odd years of the shop's existence, film stars, tycoons and politicians have joined the queue for a table. Besides regular brisket, you can order the chewier butterfly brisket (爽腩; *song laam*), and beef tendon (牛筋; *ngau gun*), served in a curry sauce with noodles.

Heirloom   EUROPEAN, MEXICAN $$

16 Map p30, B2

This great little bistro with open frontage and a cosy upper floor offers a delicious selection of European and Mexican fare, including excellent tacos (a rarity in Hong Kong, excellent or otherwise). (☏2547 8008; www.heirloomhk.com; 226 Hollywood Rd; meals from $150; ⏱10am-11pm Tue-Sat, 11am-5pm Sun; Ⓜ Sheung Wan, 🚌26)

Linguini Fini   ITALIAN, ORGANIC $

17 Map p30, E2

Another awesome choice for casual Italian – the pasta is made fresh, meats are home-cured, and produce is sourced from local organic farms. The nose-to-tail approach to pork means you get rare yummies such as fried testa and tripe cooked with tomatoes. (☏2857 1333; www.linguinifini.com; ground fl & 1st fl, L Place, 139 Queen's Rd Central; lunch/dinner from $120/200; ⏱lunch & dinner; Ⓜ Central, exit D2)

Caprice   MODERN FRENCH $$$

In spite of its opulent appearance, this restaurant, in the Four Seasons Hotel just like Lung King Heen (see 13 Map p30, F2), has a straightforward menu, masterfully created from ingredients flown in daily from France. The selections change, but experience says anything with duck, langoustine or pork belly is out of this world. If you like cheese, its artisanal cheeses, imported weekly, are arguably the best you can get in Hong Kong. (☏3196 8888; www.fourseasons.com/hong kong; Four Seasons Hotel, 8 Finance St; set lunch from $380; ⏱lunch & dinner; Ⓜ Hong Kong, exit E1)

City Hall Maxim's Palace   DIM SUM $$

18 Map p30, G3

You'll find the real Hong Kong dim-sum deal, with all its clatter and clutter, in Hong Kong City Hall, busiest on Saturday or Sunday morning. Cacophonous but delectable. (大會堂 美心皇宮; ☏2521 1303; 3rd fl, Low Block, Hong Kong City Hall, 1 Edinburgh Pl, Central; (☏11am-4.30pm & 5.30-10.45pm Mon-Sat, 9am-4.30pm & 5.30-10.45pm Sun; Ⓜ Central, exit K)

Drinking

Sevva
BAR

19 Map p30, F4

If there was a million-dollar view, it'd be the one from the balcony of this stylish number – skyscrapers so close you see their arteries of steel, with the harbour and Kowloon in the distance. At night it takes your breath away, and Sevva's cocktails are a wonderful excuse to let it happen. (☎2537 1388; www.sevva.hk; 25th fl, Prince's Bldg, 10 Chater Rd, Central; ⏰noon-midnight Mon-Thu, to 2am Fri & Sat; Ⓜ Central, exit H)

Amo Eno
WINE BAR

20 Map p30, F2

'Love wine' delivers a sophisticated wine experience, whether you're a debutant or a connoisseur. You can browse by colour, grape and price on a table with a touch-screen top, then pick your poison and the size of pour from a total of 72 bottles kept in state-of-the-art enomatic dispensers. (shop 3027, podium level 3, IFC Mall, 1 Harbour View St; Ⓜ Hong Kong, exit E)

Liberty Exchange
SPORTS BAR

21 Map p30, F3

This American bar and bistro is hugely popular with bankers and hedgies. On Friday evening it's packed with people exchanging industry gossip over cocktail, wine or beer, or watching sport on one of the big TV screens. (www.lex.hk; Two Exchange Sq,

8 Connaught Pl; ⏰noon-11pm Mon-Fri, 11.30am-10pm Sat, 11.30am-3pm Sun, happy hr 3-8pm; Ⓜ Hong Kong, exit A1)

Entertainment

Grappa's Cellar
LIVE MUSIC

22 ⭐ Map p30, F3

This subterranean Italian restaurant morphs into an indie music venue two weekends a month; see website for details. (☎2521 2322; www.elgrande.com.hk/outlets/HongKong/GrappasCellar; 1 Connaught Pl; Ⓜ Central, exit A1)

 Local Life

Hankering for Pampering?

If you ever need balm for your travellers' feet, visit **Ten Feet Tall** (Map p30, E2; ☎2971 1010; www.tenfeettall.com.hk; 20th & 21st fl, L Place, 139 Queen's Rd, Central; ⏰11am-midnight Sun-Thu, to 1am Fri & Sat), a sprawling comfort den offering indulgences from foot reflexology and shoulder massage, to hard-core pressure-point massage and aromatic oil treatments. Or try ultra-high-end **Spa at the Four Seasons** (Map p30, F2; ☎3196 8888; www.fourseasons.com; Four Seasons Hotel, 8 Finance St, Central; Ⓜ Hong Kong, exit E1), with its comprehensive range of beauty, massage and health treatments, plus ice fountain, hot cups, moxibustion and herbal cocoon room.

Hong Kong City Hall

PERFORMING ARTS

23 Map p30, G3

Built in 1962, Hong Kong City Hall is still a major cultural venue, with concert and recital halls and a theatre. (香港大會堂; ☎2921 2840, bookings 2734 9009; www.cityhall.gov.hk; Low Block, 1 Edinburgh Pl, Central; MCentral)

Shopping

Shanghai Tang

CLOTHING & ACCESSORIES

24 🔒 Map p30, F4

If you fancy a Chinese dress with a modern twist, a picture frame with an auspicious motif, or a mah-jong tile set designed in a modern chinoiserie style, this is the place to go. (上海灘; ☎2525 7333; www.shanghaitang .com; Shanghai Tang Mansion, 1 Duddell St; MCentral, exit D1)

Fook Ming Tong Tea Shop

FOOD & DRINK

Located in Two IFC (see 2 ◉ Map p30, F2), here you'll find tea-making accoutrements and carefully chosen teas of various ages and grades, from gunpowder to Nanyan Ti Guan Yin Crown Grade. Costs are anything from $10 to $9000 per 100g. (福茗堂茶莊; ☎2295 0368; shop 3006, IFC Mall, 8 Finance St; MCentral, exit A)

Blanc de Chine

CLOTHING & ACCESSORIES

This sumptuous store, in the same building as Sevva (see 19 🔒 Map p30, F2), specialises in traditional Chinese men's jackets and silk dresses for women, off the rack or made to measure. The satin bed linens are exquisite (as are the old ship's cabinets in which they are displayed). (源; ☎2104 7934; www.blancdechine.com; shop 123, Prince's Bldg; ◷10.30am-7.30pm Mon-Sat, noon-6pm Sun; MCentral, exit H)

Sin Sin Fine Art

ART

25 🔒 Map p30, C2

This eclectic gallery, owned by a fashion designer with a flair for ethnic designs, shows Hong Kong, mainland Chinese and Southeast Asian paintings and photography. (☎2858 5072; www.sinsin.com.hk; ground fl, 53-54 Sai St, Central; ◷9.30am-6.30pm Tue-Sat, 1.30-6.30pm Sun; MSheung Wan, exit A2)

Hong Kong Book Centre

BOOKS

26 🔒 Map p30, F3

This basement shop has a vast selection of books and magazines, including a mammoth number of business titles. (☎2522 7064; www.swindonbooks .com; basement, On Lok Yuen Bldg, 25 Des Voeux Rd Central, Central; ◷9am-6.30pm Mon-Fri, to 5.30pm Sat; MCentral, exit B)

◯ Local Life
Where Else to Shop in Central

Sumptuous temples to couture and conspicuous consumption prosper inside Central's swish shopping malls, where you'll also find midrange clothing brands. Take your pick from the **Princes Building** (太子大廈; Map p30, E3; www.centralhk.com; 10 Chater Rd; **M**Central, exit K), the **Landmark** (置地廣場; Map p30, E3; www.centralhk .com; 1 Pedder St; **M**Central, exit G) or the **IFC Mall** (Map p30, E2; www.ifc .com.hk; 8 Finance St; **M**Hong Kong, exit F). **Peddar Building** (Map p30, D3; 12 Peddar St, Central; **M**Central, exit H) is particularly good for fine art, while **Stanley Street** (Map p30, D3) in Central is the spot for quality cameras. For an only-in-Hong-Kong experience, visit **Li Yuen Street East and West** (Map p30, D2), two narrow alleyways that link Des Voeux Rd Central with Queen's Rd Central, for a jumble of inexpensive clothing, handbags and jewellery.

Homeless   FURNITURE, ACCESSORIES

27 🅐 Map p30, D2

At these lifestyle stores, furniture, clothing and a range of retro and idiosyncratic accessories are tossed together attractively in an industrial setting. Watch out for products embellished with the fantastical drawings of Carrie Chau, a talented local designer. (☎2581 1160; www.homelessconcept.com; 28 Gough St, Sheung Wan; **M**Sheung Wan, exit A2)

Ranee K   CLOTHING

28 🅐 Map p30, D2

US-trained local designer Ranee Kok is known for her combinations of dramatic prints and textures, and deft adoption of the cuts, patterns and styles from both the East and West in her evening and ready-to-wear lines. (郭翠華; ☎2108 4068; www.raneek.com; 25 Aberdeen St, Sheung Wan; ⏰11.30am-8pm; **M**Sheung Wan, exit A2)

Explore

Hong Kong Island: Lan Kwai Fong & Soho

Lan Kwai Fong and Soho form the party epicentre of Hong Kong. Lan Kwai Fong is an alleyway dog-legging south and west from D'Aguilar St; as an area it also covers D'Aguilar St, Wo On Lane, Wing Wah Lane and Wyndham St. The crowd here is relatively young, middle class and cosmopolitan. Soho ('south of Hollywood Rd') has art galleries and antique shops, besides dining and drinking hotspots.

The Sights in a Day

☀ Take the Peak Tram up to **Victoria Peak** (p58) and spend a couple of hours exploring its leafy walks, stopping for photos and ice cream, and checking out the shops. On your way down, have an early dim-sum lunch at Michelin-crowned **Luk Yu Teahouse** (p49).

☀ Browse the **art galleries and antique shops** on Hollywood Rd (p56), pausing at the **Central Police Station Compound** (p47) to peek over its walls. For the next hour or two, partake of a movable feast of street life and history on the **Central-Midlevels Escalator** (p47). Hop off to explore **Graham Street Market** (p47) and stock up on good-quality Chinese condiments and exotic snacks at **Kowloon Soy Company** (p57). Then join slacking office workers for afternoon tea at 1950s *cha chaan tang* (teahouse) **Lan Fong Yuen** (p51), or enjoy organic coffee and vegan pastries at **Life Cafe** (p49).

☾ Have dinner at **Ser Wong Fun** (p51), followed by a foot massage at **Happy Foot Reflexology** (p48) next door. Then go bar crawling (p44), stopping at **Brickhouse** (p50) for tacos to soak up the alcohol.

🔍 **Local Life**

LKF & Soho Bar Crawl (p44)

 Best of Hong Kong

Eating

Luk Yu Teahouse (p49)

Sushi Kuu (p50)

Gold by Harlan Goldstein (p49)

Life Cafe (p49)

Drinking

Club 71 (p45)

Bar 42 (p52)

Flying Winemaker (p45)

The Globe (p52)

Angel's Share (p52)

Getting There

🚌 **Bus** Bus 26 runs along Hollywood Rd.

Ⓜ **MTR** Central station (Island and Tsuen Wan lines).

Local Life
LKF & Soho Bar Crawl

Here are some of the more charismatic venues in LKF and Soho favoured by seasoned local revellers. While some may appeal to wine connoisseurs, others to cocktail or culture buffs, all of the selections command enough charm, booze and atmosphere to give anyone a memorable (even if not fully remembered) night out.

❶ 'Secret' Garden

An open secret of sorts, this **amphitheatre** (Lok Hing Lane Park, Wo On Lane, Lan Kwai Fong; Ⓜ Central, exit D2) is the hang-out of young expats who bring some drinks here to shoot the breeze. Come for relief from the noise and crowds, and to meet people.

❷ Shake a Leg African Style

Venture into Africa at **Makumba** (☏ 2522 0544; www.makumba.hk; 2nd fl, Ho

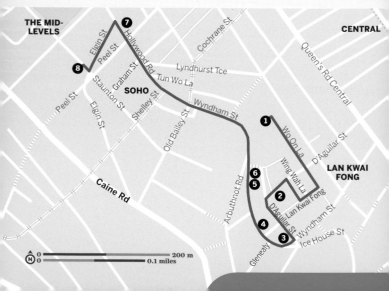

Lee Commercial Bldg, 38-44 D'Aguilar St, Lan Kwai Fong; ⏰6pm-late; Ⓜ Central, exit D2), saturated with earthy vibes and pulsating rhythms, with a spacious dance floor where a predominantly African crowd sways to live Afro-jazz.

❸ Meet a Winemaker

Flying Winemaker (http://eddiemcdougall .com; 31 Wyndham St, Lan Kwai Fong; ⏰happy hr 3-8pm; Ⓜ Central, exit D2) is a smart corner bar opened by local-born Eddie McDougall, who's out to alter people's impression of wine as an uppity drink sipped from delicate wine glasses. Try one of his handcrafted varietals or a Lebanese vintage from no less than a plastic cup (it has wine glasses too).

❹ Play Ball While You Drink

Skipped the gym? **Tazmania Ballroom** (☎2801 5009; www.tazmaniaballroom.com; 1st fl, LKF Tower, 33 Wyndham St, Lan Kwai Fong; ⏰5am-late; Ⓜ Central, exit D2) whips out ping-pong tables every Tuesday, Thursday and Saturday. The dress code, however, is casual glam, not Chinese national team. Shoot pool with bankers at a gold-plated table or join model types for some verbal back-and-forth on the balcony.

❺ Chill, Frolic, Repeat

Sophisticated **Tivo** (☎2116 8055; www .aqua.com.hk; 43-55 Wyndham St, Lan Kwai Fong; ⏰noon-2am Mon-Sat; Ⓜ Central, exit D2) delights with open frontage, an exuberant crowd and aperitivo-type snacks. On the first and third Sunday

of the month, lovely drag hostesses take over from 7pm and whip up the action for the Tivo Tea Dance.

❻ Mojitos in Ancient China

Next door is 'Cloud's Residence' or **Yun Fu** (雲府; ☎2116 8855; www.aqua .com.hk; basement, 43-55 Wyndham St, Lan Kwai Fong; ⏰noon-2am Mon-Sat; Ⓜ Central, exit D2); in the glow of lanterns, make out period furniture, carved doors and winding corridors while sipping your fresh-fruit cocktail. Tunes mixed by a DJ.

❼ Meet Local Activists

Named after a protest that took place on 1 July 2003 against an article that would limit freedom of speech, **Club 71** (☎2858 7071; basement, 67 Hollywood Rd, Soho; ⏰3pm-2am Mon-Sat, 6pm-1am Sun; happy hr 3-9pm; Ⓜ Central, exit D2) is where activists and artists gather for beer and music sessions. Out front, revolutionaries plotted to overthrow the Qing dynasty a hundred years ago. Enter the alley at 67 Hollywood Rd.

❽ Daiquiris in a 'Bordello'

At the end of Staunton St in Soho you'll see a place with velvet curtains and no signage. **Feather Boa** (☎2857 2586, 38 Staunton St, Soho; ⏰9pm-midnight; 🚌26), your final stop, is a dimly lit, bordello-like chamber, with candles, gold-plated mirrors and antique furniture. The strawberry-chocolate daiquiris are popular with the European clientele. Bring ID.

A · B · C · D

N 0 — 200 m
0 — 0.1 miles

SHEUNG WAN THE MID-LEVELS

Jervois St

Queen's Rd Central

Wing Kut St

Gilman's Bazaar

Des Voeux Rd Central

CENTRAL

Kau U Fong

Gough St

Jubilee St

Queen Victoria St

Queen's Rd Central

Man Yee La

Pottinger St

Li Yuen St West

Li Yuen St East

Douglas St

Mee Lun St

Aberdeen St

Gage St

Peel St

Wellington St

Cochrane St

34

Graham Street Market

2

Happy Foot Reflexology

4

Hollywood Rd

Elgin St

9 28 27

15

30

16

SOHO

Graham St

Gutzlaff St

14

13

Tun Wo La

Lyndhurst Tce

Stanley St

Wellington St

Central-Midlevels Escalator

3 33

Ezra's La

21 17

37

1

Hollywood Rd

24

35

6

36

Peel St

Elgin St

26 22

23

7

Staunton St

Central Police Station Compound

Wo On La

12

19

Shelley St

29

Wing Wah La

D'Aguilar St

LAN KWAI FONG

18

11

Old Bailey St

Chancery La

32

Caine Rd

Arbuthnot Rd

Wyndham St

Sense of Touch

5

20

8

31

D'Aguilar St

Lan Kwai Fong

10

25

Wyndham St

Gleneally

Albert Rd

Ice House St

For reviews see

- ◉ Sights   p47
- ✕ Eating   p49
- 🍷 Drinking   p52
- ★ Entertainment p54
- 🛍 Shopping   p56

Sights

Central Police Station Compound

HISTORIC BUILDING

1 Map p46, C3

This disused police–magistracy–prison compound, comprising 27 buildings in Victorian and Edwardian styles modelled after London's Old Bailey, offered one-stop, handcuff-to-leg-iron service before 'streamlining' was fashionable. It's usually closed except when hired for events, but there are plans to turn it into an art complex with gallery, cinema and museum by 2014. (中區警署; www.centralpolicestation.org.hk; 10 Hollywood Rd; 🚍26)

Graham Street Market

MARKET

2 Map p46, B2

The market stalls and open-air canteens centred on Graham St are a compelling destination to stroll around to get a close look at the exotic produce that Hong Kong prides itself on selling and consuming. Preserved 'thousand year' eggs and fresh tofu curd scooped from wooden tubs are just some of the items on display. (Graham St, Soho; admission free; Ⓜ Central, exit D2)

Take a Break Have a Hong Kong–style tea at **Lan Fong Yuen** (p51).

Top Tip

Booking & Tipping

It's strongly advisable to book ahead in all but the cheapest restaurants, especially on Friday and Saturday nights. Most places above midrange add a 10% service charge to the bill. If the service at a top-end restaurant is outstanding, you might consider adding another 5% or 10% on top of the service charge. At midrange places, $5 to $20 is sufficient.

Central-Midlevels Escalator

ESCALATOR

3 Map p46, B3

Embark on the world's longest (800m) covered outdoor people-mover and let the streets unveil – Stanley and Wellington with their glamour and tradition; Gage and Lyndhurst with bars and boutiques where florists and prostitutes once hawked their wares; Hollywood, Hong Kong's second-oldest street; Staunton, whose porcelain shops made way for Soho; then Shelley, named unromantically after an infamous auditor-general. (中環至半山自動扶梯; from cnr Cochrane St & Queen's Rd Central to Caine Rd; admission free; ⏱ down 6-10am, up 10.30am-midnight; Ⓜ Central, exit C)

Take a Break Enjoy a raw vegan ice cream or vegan flatbread at **Mana! Fast**

Graham Street Market (p47)

Slow Food (Map p46, C3; http://mana.hk; 92 Wellington St, Lan Kwai Fong; meals $90-200; ⏺10.30am-10pm Mon-Sat, to 9pm Sun).

Happy Foot Reflexology

HEALTH

4 Map p46, C2

Give your walk-weary tootsies (or other bits and pieces) a pampering at the aptly named Happy Foot. Foot/body massages start at $198 for 50 minutes. A pedicure costs $180. (知足樂; ☎2544 1010; www.happyfoot.hk; 11th & 13th fl, Jade Centre, 98-102 Wellington St, Central; ⏺10am-midnight; Ⓜ Central, exit F)

Sense of Touch

HEALTH & FITNESS

5 Map p46, C4

This award-winning spa offers every conceivable form of treatment including a dark ale beer bath and a wine bath for two. A straightforward 90-minute bath and massage will set you back $1100. (☎2526 6918; www.sense oftouch.com.hk; 1st-5th fl, 52 D'Aguilar St, Lan Kwai Fong; ⏺10am-9pm Mon-Fri, to 7pm Sat & Sun; Ⓜ Central, exit D2)

Eating

Luk Yu Teahouse CANTONESE $$

6 Map p46, D3

This Michelin-crowned teahouse (c 1933), known for its masterful cooking and Eastern art-deco decor, was once the haunt of opera artists, writers and painters (including the creator of one exorbitant ink-and-brush gracing a wall), who gave recitals and discussed national fate over steaming dim sum. Today some of the same waiters that served the tousled glamourati will pour your tea in the same pleasantly irreverent manner. (陸羽茶室; ☎ 2523 5464; 24-26 Stanley St, Lan Kwai Fong; meals from $250; ⏰ 7am-10pm; ♿; M Central, exit D2)

Life Cafe VEGETARIAN, WESTERN $

7 Map p46, B3

Life serves fantastic vegan salads, cakes and dishes free from gluten, wheat, garlic – you name it – over three floors stylishly decked out in reclaimed teak and recycled copper-domed lamps. The ground-floor counter has guilt-free goodies to take away. (☎ 2810 9777; www.lifecafe.com.hk; 10 Shelley St, Soho; meals from $100; ⏰ noon-10pm; ♥ ♿; 🚌 26)

Gold by Harlan Goldstein MODERN ITALIAN $$$

8 Map p46, C4

Michelin-recommended and a darling of food critics, Gold is known for its brilliant slant on Italian cuisine. Ingredients may be French, Spanish or Japanese, but are expertly prepared with Italian finesse, and served in a luminous brasserie-like setting. The semibuffet lunch ($270 per person) is generous, and for an extra $190 you can also order Gold's signature dish:

Top Tip

Budget Bites

Western fast-food chains are everywhere but for something slightly more exotic, try these local chains:

Café de Coral (www.cafedecoral.com) A huge range of Chinese dishes; free wi-fi

Genki Sushi (www.genkisushi.com.sg) Cheap but reasonable sushi, carousel-style.

Maxim's (www.maxims.com.hk) Canto dishes with a focus on Chinese barbecued meat.

Mix (www.mix-world.com) Smoothies, wraps and salads, and free internet.

Oliver's (www.olivers-supersandwiches.com) Sandwiches and salads.

Top Tip

Stubbed Out

Smoking has been banned in all bars, restaurants, shopping malls, museums, public transport, even beaches and parks, in Hong Kong; but you can light up in 'al fresco' areas. Some bars, however, will risk getting fined in order to attract more customers – you know which ones they are by the ashtray nonchalantly left on tables. An exception to the ban is on cross-border trains to mainland China, where you can smoke in the restaurant car and the vestibules at either end of the cars, but not in the main seating area.

handcrafted spaghetti with lobster. (☎2869 9986; www.gold-dining.com; level 2, LKF Tower, 33 Wyndham St, Lan Kwai Fong; lunch $300-800, dinner $800-1000; ☺lunch & dinner Mon-Sat; ⓂCentral, exit D2)

Vbest Tea House

CANTONESE $

9 Map p46, A3

Tucked away on a steep street off Hollywood Rd, this understated family-run restaurant serves MSG-free comfort food. The owners' children grew up on this, so you can't go too wrong. We recommend the pork-and-chive wontons and prawns with rice vermicelli. (緻好茶館; ☎3104 0890; www.vbest.com.hk; 17 Elgin St, Soho; lunch from $80, dinner from $180; ☺noon-3pm & 6-11pm Mon-Sat; ✐; ⓂCentral, exit C, Central-Midlevels Escalator)

Sushi Kuu

JAPANESE $$$

10 Map p46, D4

If you order the *omakase* (meaning 'I'll leave it to you') at our favourite sushi bar, the chef will serve you a multicourse meal prepared with the sweetest fruits of the sea he has available. Starting from $950 per person, it doesn't come cheap, but the quality is impeccable. The lunch sets (from $250) are also much raved about. Booking essential. (壽司喰; ☎2971 0180; 1st fl, Wellington Pl, 2-8 Wellington St, Lan Kwai Fong; ☺noon-11pm Mon-Thu & Sun, noon-12.30am Fri & Sat; ⓂCentral, exit D2)

Brickhouse

MEXICAN $$

11 Map p46, D4

Currently the go-to place for good Mexican food, Brickhouse is heaving every night with hipsters who can't get enough of the tacos made with handcrafted tortillas, and fresh-fish ceviches. It doesn't take reservations, so swivel a cocktail at the bar (6pm to 2am Monday to Wednesday, to 4am Thursday to Saturday) and admire the street-art decoration while you wait. (☎2810 0560; www.brickhouse.com.hk; 20A D'Aguilar St, Lan Kwai Fong; meals from $350; ☺6pm-midnight Mon-Wed, to 2am Thu-Sat; ⓂCentral, exit D2)

Yung Kee

CANTONESE, DIM SUM $$

12 Map p46, D4

This long-standing institution is frequented by families, celebrities and Central's office workers. Its roast

Luk Yu Teahouse (p49)

goose, made from fowls raised in the restaurant's own farm, has been the talk of the town since 1942. (鏞記; ☑2522 1624; 32-40 Wellington St, Lan Kwai Fong; lunch $80-300, dinner from $380; ⊙lunch & dinner; Ⓜ Central, exit D2)

Ser Wong Fun
CANTONESE $

 13 Map p46, C3

This snake-soup specialist whips up old Cantonese dishes that are as tantalising as its celebrated broth, and the packed tables attest to it. Many regulars come just for the homemade pork-liver sausage infused with rose wine – perfect over a bowl of immacu

late white rice, on a red tablecloth. Booking advised. (蛇王芬; ☑2543 1032; 30 Cochrane St, Soho; meals $70-150; ⊙11am-10.30pm; Ⓜ Central, exit D1)

Lan Fong Yuen
TEA CAFE $

14 Map p46, B3

Busy Lan Fong Yuen (1952) is a *cha chaan tang* serving pseudo-Western food to those who couldn't afford the real deal. It's said to have invented the strong and silky 'pantyhose milk tea', more than a thousand cups of which are sold daily alongside pork-chop buns, tossed noodles and other hasty tastics. Due to its small size and low

Local Life
Gay-Friendly Bars

While Hong Kong's gay scene may not have the visibility of that of New York, it's made huge strides. When homosexual acts between consenting adults were decriminalised in 1991, there were only a couple of speakeasies. Today there are some 30 bars and clubs. **DYMK** (Map p46, C4; 16 Arbuthnot Rd, Central; ☺6pm-4am; MCentral, exit D2) caters to discerning professionals lounging in stylishly lit booths. **T:me** (Map p46, B2; www.time-bar.com; ☺6pm-2am Mon-Sat; MCentral, exit D2), in an alley off Hollywood Rd, is tiny but chic. Cocktail bar **Volume** (Map p46, A2; 83-85 Hollywood Rd, Central; ☺6pm-4am; MCentral, exit D2) pumps out sounds from '80s hits to the latest dance genres. See free monthly gay magazine **Dim Sum** (http://dimsum-hk.com) for listings.

prices there's a cover charge of $20. (蘭芳園; ☏2544 3895, 2854 0731; 2 Gage St, Soho; ☺7am-6pm Mon-Sat; MCentral, exit D1)

Drinking

Bar 42   BAR

15 Map p46, A3

The former Barco is now Bar 42, but it hasn't lost its appeal. The staff are still wonderful, and the cozy lounge

continues to attract a cool mix of journalists, designers and young entrepreneurs, local and expat. (42 Staunton St, Soho; ☺happy hr 4-8pm; MCentral, exit D2)

The Globe   GASTROPUB

16 Map p46, B3

This massive pub is one of the few watering holes that serves T8, the first cask-conditioned ale brewed in Hong Kong, alongside more than a hundred beers, including rare imported brews such as de Kronick, which is on tap. (45-53 Graham St, Soho; ☺happy hr 9am-8pm; MCentral, exit D1)

Angel's Share   WHISKY BAR

17 Map p46, B3

One of Hong Kong's best whisky bars, this clubby place has more than a hundred whiskies from the world over. One of these (a 23-year-old Macallan) comes straight out of a large 180-litre oak barrel placed in the centre of the room. (☏2805 8388; www.angelsshare.hk; 2nd fl, Amber Lodge, 23 Hollywood Rd, Lan Kwai Fong; ☺3pm-2am Mon-Thu, to 3am Fri & Sat; MCentral, exit D1)

Bit Point   GERMAN BAR

18 Map p46, C4

Smack in the thick of the LKF action, German-style Bit Point has a good selection of German beers on tap and a sausage platter to stoke your thirst. The amicable Eurasian owner, Cindy, is happy to give you sightseeing recommendations in Hong Kong. Take a table by the entrance if you want to smoke. (ground fl, 31 D'Aguilar St; ☺happy hr 4-9pm; Ⓜ Central, exit D2)

Tastings   WINE BAR

19 Map p46, D4

Awash in blue light, this cool subterranean den has enomatic wine dispensers that allow you to sample – by sips, half-glasses or full glasses – a wide range of vintages (40) without having to open the bottle. The selection changes but always includes rare bottles from Lebanon or Israel. (✆2523 6282; www.tastings.hk; basement, Yuen Yick Bldg, 27 & 29 Wellington St, Lan Kwai Fong; ☺5pm-2am Mon-Sat; Ⓜ Central, exit D2)

Dragon-I   BAR

20 Map p46, C4

Opened by the owner of a modelling agency, this place has both an indoor bar and a huge terrace filled with caged songbirds. Go after midnight and you'll see Ukranian models and Cantopop stars sipping Krug, air kissing and posing. Dress to kill or go early if you want to be let in. (upper ground fl, the Centrium, 60 Wyndham St; ☺happy hr 3-9pm Mon-Sat (terrace); Ⓜ Central, exit D2)

Top Tip
For Lesbians
Hong Kong's premier lesbian organisation **Les Peches** (✆9101 8001; lespechesinfo@yahoo.com) has events for lesbians, bisexual women and their friends, including monthly club nights and a popular annual junk-trip flotilla event.

Solas   BAR

If the nasty man wouldn't let you into Dragon-I upstairs (see **20** Map p46, C4), never mind. This relaxed, friendly, Irish-owned place, where a DJ spins chilled lounge sounds and the cocktails pack a punch, is more than a consolation prize. (✆3162 3710; www .solas.com.hk; 60 Wyndham St; ☺noon-2am Mon-Sat; Ⓜ Central, exit D2)

Gecko Lounge   BAR, LIVE MUSIC

21 Map p46, C3

Gecko is a relaxed hideout that attracts a fun crowd, especially to its live jazz sessions on Tuesday and Wednesday. The well-hidden DJ mixes good grooves with kooky Parisian tunes at weekends. There's a great wine list. Enter from Ezra's Lane off Cochrane or Pottinger Sts. (✆2537 4680; lower ground fl, 15-19 Hollywood Rd, Soho; ☺4pm-2am Mon-Thu, 4pm-4am Fri & Sat, happy hr 6-9pm; Ⓜ Central, exit D1)

Staunton's Wine Bar & Café

BAR, CAFE

22 🎧 Map p46, B3

Staunton's is swish, cool and on the ball, with decent wine and a lovely terrace. For eats, there's light fare downstairs and a modern international restaurant called Scirocco above. (10-12 Staunton St, Soho; ⏱happy hr 5-9pm; 🚍13, 26, 40M)

Peak Cafe Bar

BAR, CAFE

23 🎧 Map p46, B4

The fixtures and fittings of the much-missed Peak Cafe, from 1947, have moved down the hill to this comfy bar with super cocktails and excellent nosh. The only thing missing is the view. (山頂餐廳; 📞2140 6877; 9-13 Shelley St, Soho; ⏱11am-2am Mon-Sat, 11am-midnight Sun, happy hr 5-8pm; 🚍13, 26, 40M)

Entertainment

Backstage Live Restaurant

LIVE MUSIC

24 ⭐ Map p46, C3

Gigs of new indie, alternative and post-punk from Hong Kong and overseas are played four or more nights a week at Backstage Live, a name synonymous with independent

LONELY PLANET/GETTY IMAGES ©

Dragon-I (p53)

music. Check the website for the latest. (✆2167 8985; www.backstagelive.hk; 1st fl, Somptueux Central, 52-54 Wellington St, Lan Kwai Fong; ⏰11.30am-late Mon-Fri, 6.30pm-late Sat; Ⓜ Central, exit D1)

Fringe Club
LIVE MUSIC, THEATRE

25 ⭐ Map p46, D5

The Fringe, a friendly and eclectic venue on the border of Lan Kwai Fong, has original music in its gallery-bar from 9.30pm on Friday and Saturday, with jazz, rock and world music getting the most airplay. The intimate theatres, each seating up to a hundred, host eclectic local and international performances. (藝穗會; ✆2521 7251, theatre bookings 2521 9126; www.hkfringeclub.com; ground & 1st fl, Dairy Farm Bldg, 2 Lower Albert Rd, Lan Kwai Fong; ⏰noon-midnight Mon-Thu, noon-3am Fri & Sat; Ⓜ Central, exit G)

Takeout Comedy Club
COMEDY

26 ⭐ Map p46, A3

In need of some LOL? Hong Kong's first full-time comedy club, founded by Chinese-American Jameson Gong, has stand-up and improv acts in English, Cantonese and Mandarin. It also hosts visiting comedians from overseas. (✆6220 4436; www.takeoutcomedy .com; basement, 34 Elgin St, Soho; 🚌26)

Joyce Is Not Here
LIVE MUSIC

27 ⭐ Map p46, B3

This super-chilled cafe-bar in reds, whites and blacks has something for everyone – from poetry readings and live music to Sunday brunch. It's one of those rare places that are artsy (writers and musicians hang out here every evening) and homey (the owner's young family is always here) at the same time. Joyce is closed on Monday. (✆2851 2999; www.joycebaker design.com; 38-44 Peel St, Soho; ⏰4.30pm-late Tue-Fri, 1.30pm-late Sat & Sun; 🚌13, 26, 40M)

Top Tip
What's On Where & When

Artslink (www.hkac.org.hk) A monthly guide with listings of performances, exhibitions and art-house films.

bc magazine (www.bcmagazine.net) A free biweekly guide to Hong Kong's entertainment and partying scene.

HK Magazine (http://hk.asia-city.com) A free and comprehensive entertainment listings magazine.

Time Out (www.timeout.com.hk) An authoritative fortnightly guide to what's on.

Urbtix (☎2111 5999; www.urbtix.gov.hk) Bookings for most cultural events online or by phone.

Cityline (☎2314 4228; www.cityline.com.hk) Affiliate of Urbtix; also good for bookings.

Peel Fresco
LIVE JAZZ

28 Map p46, A3

Charming Peel Fresco has live jazz six nights a week, with local and overseas acts performing on a small but spectacular stage next to teetering Renaissance-style paintings. The action starts around 9.30pm, but go at 9pm to secure a seat. (☎2540 2064; www.peelfresco.com; 49 Peel St, Soho; ☉5pm-late Mon-Sat; 🚌13, 26, 40M)

Skylark Lounge
LIVE JAZZ

29 Map p46, C4

There's live jazz every night of the week (and the odd comedy gig) at this bar above a 7-Eleven store. Performances begin at 9.30pm and happy hour at 8.30pm. Check website for band list. (☎2801 6018; www.skylarklounge.hk; 1st fl, Parekh House, 63 Wyndham St, Lan Kwai Fong; ☉8.30pm-late; Ⓜ Central, exit D1)

Shopping

Arch Angel Antiques
ANTIQUES, ART

30 Map p46, B2

Though its specialities are ancient porcelain and tombware, Arch Angel packs a lot more into its three floors: everything from mah-jong sets and terracotta horses to palatial furniture. (☎2851 6848; 53-55 Hollywood Rd, Lan Kwai Fong; ☉9.30am-6.30pm; 🚌26)

Grotto Fine Art
FINE ART

31 Map p46, C5

This exquisite gallery, founded by a scholar in modern and contemporary Hong Kong art, is one of very few that represents predominantly local artists. The small but excellent selection of works shown ranges from painting and sculpture to ceramics and mixed media. Prices are quite reasonable too. (嘉圖現代藝術有限公司; ☎2121 2270; www.grottofineart.com; 2nd fl, 31C-D Wyndham St, Lan Kwai Fong; ☉11am-7pm Mon-Sat; Ⓜ Central, exit G)

10 Chancery Lane Gallery

ART

32 🔒 Map p46, B4

Located on Chancery Lane, this gallery focuses on thought-provoking works by promising Asian, mainland Chinese and Hong Kong artists, and runs seminars and art walks. (☎2810 0065; www.10chancerylanegallery.com; ground fl, 10 Chancery Lane, Lan Kwai Fong; ⏰10am-6pm Mon-Sat; Ⓜ Central, exit D2)

Honeychurch Antiques

ANTIQUES

33 🔒 Map p46, B3

This fine shop specialises in antique Chinese furniture, jewellery, and antique English silver. There's a wide range of stock, with items from the early Chinese dynasties right up to the 20th century. (☎2543 2433; 29 Hollywood Rd, Lan Kwai Fong; ⏰9am-6.30pm Mon-Sat; 🚇26)

Kowloon Soy Company

CHINESE CONDIMENTS

34 🔒 Map p46, C2

The shop (c 1917) for artisanal soy sauce and Chinese condiments; also sells preserved eggs (*pei darn,* 皮蛋) and pickled ginger (*suen geung,* 酸薑). Did you know that young red wines taste fuller-bodied when consumed with preserved eggs? Just try it. (九龍醬園; ☎2544 3695; www.kowloonsoy.com; 9 Graham St, Soho; ⏰8am-6.15pm Mon-Fri, to 6pm Sat; Ⓜ Central, exit D1)

Lulu Cheung

CLOTHING

35 🔒 Map p46, C3

Local designer Lulu Cheung makes sophisticated casualwear, work clothes and evening gowns for the urban woman, using natural fabrics such as wool, cotton, silk and linen, in whites and earth tones. The look is subtle and feminine without being prudish. (☎2537 7515; www.lulucheung.com.hk; Shop B, 50 Wellington St, Lan Kwai Fong; ⏰10am-8pm Sun-Thu, to 9pm Fri & Sat; Ⓜ Central, exit D2)

Photo Scientific

PHOTOGRAPHIC EQUIPMENT

36 🔒 Map p46, D3

This shop is the favourite of Hong Kong's professional photographers. You may find cheaper equipment elsewhere, but Photo Scientific has a rock-solid reputation, with labelled prices and no bargaining. (攝影科學; ☎2525 0550; ground fl, Eurasia Bldg, 6 Stanley St, Lan Kwai Fong; ⏰9am-7pm Mon-Sat; Ⓜ Central, exit D2)

Wattis Fine Art

ANTIQUES

37 🔒 Map p46, B3

No other shop in Hong Kong has a better collection of antique maps for sale than this place; the selection of old photographs of Hong Kong and Macau is also very impressive. Enter from Old Bailey St. (☎2524 5302; www.wattis.com.hk; 2nd fl, 20 Hollywood Rd, Soho; ⏰10.30am-6pm Mon-Sat; 🚇26)

Top Sights
Victoria Peak

Getting There

🚌 Bus 15 to the summit (40 minutes); bus 15C or 12S to Peak Tram Lower Terminus

🚋 Peak Tram Lower Terminus, 33 Garden Rd, Central (single/return $28/40; every 10 to 15 minutes, 7am-midnight)

Standing at 552m, Victoria Peak is the highest point on Hong Kong Island, and the best way to reach it is by taking the gravity-defying Peak Tram, Hong Kong's oldest thrill-ride (125 years). Rising almost vertically above the high-rises nearby, Asia's oldest funicular clanks it way up the hillside to finish, after eight minutes, at the Peak Tower. On clear days and nights, the views from the summit are spectacular.

Peak Tower

Don't Miss

Peak Tram Historical Gallery

This **gallery** (free admission for passengers; ⊘7am midnight) at the Lower Terminus has exhibits illustrating the Peak Tram's history. Until 1940 the tram was used exclusively by Westerners, their servants, and soldiers; Chinese were barred from the Peak. Unthinkable today, but it was already an improvement: in pre-tram days, Peakies' only mode of transport were sedan chairs carried by Chinese 'chairmen'.

Victoria Peak Garden

Some 500m to the northwest of the Peak Tram's Upper Terminus, up steep Mt Austin Rd, is the site of the old governor's summer lodge, which was burned to the ground by the Japanese during WWII. The beautiful gardens have been restored, however, and refurbished with faux-Victorian gazebos, benches, sundials and stone pillars.

Nature Walks

The dappled 3.5km circuit trail formed by Harlech Rd on the south, just outside the Peak Lookout, and Lugard Rd which it runs into, takes about 45 minutes to cover. A further 2km along Peak Rd will lead you to Pok Fu Lam Reservoir Rd. Hatton Rd on the western slope goes all the way down to the University of Hong Kong in Pok Fu Lam.

Peak Tower

This anvil-shaped **building** (凌霄閣; ⊘10am-11pm Mon-Fri, 8am-11pm Sat & Sun) at the summit makes a good grandstand for views of the city. It has an outpost of **Madame Tussauds** (☑2849 6966; adult/child $170/100; ⊘10am-10pm), with eerie wax likenesses of celebrities, and on Level 5, an open-air **viewing terrace** (adult/child $30/15).

☑2522 0922

www.thepeak.com.hk

Victoria Peak, Hong Kong Island

admission free

☑ Top Tips

▶ The seats on the right side of the tram carriage going up have much better views.

▶ The Peak Galleria, adjoining the Peak Tower atop the Peak Tram Upper Terminus, has an admission-free viewing deck that's larger than the one in the tower.

✕ Take a Break

Head to the **Peak Lookout** (☑2849 1000; 121 Peak Rd; ⊘10.30am-midnight Mon-Fri, 8.30am-1am Sat, 8.30am-midnight Sun), at the road junction next to the Peak Tower, for solid European and British-Indian fare.

Explore

Hong Kong Island: Admiralty, Wan Chai & Causeway Bay

Quiet Admiralty offers class over quantity, whether it be shopping, sights or dining. To its east, Wan Chai is a seat of culture, a show-case for folk traditions and a nightlife guru, not to mention Hong Kong's most versatile kitchen. In the shopping hub of Causeway Bay, restaurants and department stores jockey for space with a racecourse and a cemetery.

The Sights in a Day

Pay a leisurely 2½-hour visit to **Hong Kong Park** (p62) and the **Asia Society Hong Kong Centre** (p70). Stroll through **Pacific Place** (p81) mall, browsing the shops, as you make your way back downhill. Have lunch at **La Creperie** (p75).

Spend two hours exploring the 'old Wan Chai' area: **Pak Tai Temple** (p70), **Hung Shing Temple** (p70), **Hong Kong House of Stories** (p71) and the vicinity. Continue your journey north to Hennessy Rd, shopping for gadgets at the **Wan Chai Computer Centre** (p82) and soaking up the vibes at **Southorn Playground** (p66) next to it. If you like, pay a visit to the **Hong Kong Convention & Exhibition Centre** (p72) and the **Hong Kong Arts Centre** (p72) right by the harbour. Then tram it to Causeway Bay to shop for the rest of the afternoon.

Have dinner at **Iroha** (p67) in Causeway Bay or **Old Bazaar Kitchen** (p75) in Wan Chai, then spend the rest of the night bar-hopping in Wan Chai.

Top Sights

Hong Kong Park (p62)

Happy Valley Racecourse (p64)

Local Life

Wan Chai Breather (p66)

Best of Hong Kong

Eating

Yin Yang (p73)

Old Bazaar Kitchen (p75)

Manor Seafood Restaurant (p75)

Drinking

b.a.r. Executive Bar (p77)

The Pawn (p77)

Getting There

M MTR Admiralty, Wan Chai, Causeway Bay and Tin Hau stations.

Tram Eastbound along Queensway, Johnston Rd and Hennessy Rd.

Bus Admiralty bus station below Queensway Plaza for buses around Hong Kong Island; buses 5, 5B and 26 for Yee Wo St (Causeway Bay). Green Minibus 40 along Tang Lung St and Yee Woo St (Causeway Bay).

Top Sights
Hong Kong Park

Designed to look anything but natural, Hong Kong Park is one of the most unusual parks in the world, emphasising artificial creations such as its fountain plaza, conservatory, artificial ponds and waterfalls (a favourite of the newly-weds from the marriage registry within the park), children's playground and taichi garden. For all its artifice, the 8-hectare park is beautiful and, with a wall of skyscrapers on one side and mountains on the other, makes for dramatic photographs.

◉ Map p68, A3

香港公園

☏ 2521 5041

www.lcsd.gov.hk/parks/hkp/en/index.php

19 Cotton Tree Dr, Admiralty

admission free

◷ 6am-11pm

Ⓜ Admiralty, exit C1

Don't Miss

Edward Youde Aviary

The park's highlight, this **aviary** (尤德觀鳥園; ☺9am-5pm) is home to more than 600 birds, representing around 90 species. Designed like a rainforest, it has a wooden bridge suspended 10m above the ground, eye level with tree branches. The **Forsgate Conservatory** (☺9am-5pm), on the slope overlooking the park, is the largest in Southeast Asia.

Flagstaff House Museum of Tea Ware

At the park's northernmost tip is this **museum** (茶具文物館; admission free; ☺10am-5pm Wed-Mon). Built in 1846, it is the oldest colonial building in Hong Kong still standing in its original spot. The museum houses a collection of antique Chinese tea ware: brewing trays, sniffing cups and teapots made of porcelain or purple clay.

KS Lo Gallery

The **KS Lo Gallery** (羅桂祥茶藝館; ☎2869 0690; 10 Cotton Tree Dr; admission free; ☺10am-5pm Wed-Mon), in a building southeast of the museum, contains rare Chinese ceramics and stone seals collected by the gallery's eponymous benefactor.

Hong Kong Visual Arts Centre

On the eastern edge of the park, the **Hong Kong Visual Arts Centre** (香港視覺藝術中心; 7A Kennedy Rd; admission free; ☺10am-9pm Wed-Mon), housed in the Cassels Block of the former Victoria Barracks, supports local artists and stages exhibitions.

☑ Top Tips

▶ There's a crafts fair (noon to 6pm Saturday and Sunday) outside the Museum of Tea Ware featuring handicrafts for sale and calligraphy and paper-cut art demos.

▶ Lock Cha Tea Shop (p63) has Chinese music performances or tea talks on Sunday (4pm to 6pm), but you'll need to reserve a seat (see website for details).

✕ Take a Break

Recharge over tea and vegetarian dim sum at classy **Lock Cha Tea Shop** (樂茶軒; Map p68, A3; ☎2801 7177; www .lockcha.com; ground fl, KS Lo Gallery; per portion $15-28; ☺10am-10pm), but book ahead if you're going for lunch or dinner. Carnivores may prefer **L16** (Map p68, A3; ☎2522 6333; www.l16 .com.hk; 19 Cotton Tree Dr; ☺11am-11pm) for its Thai snacks and grilled meats.

Top Sights
Happy Valley Racecourse

Horse racing is Hong Kong's most popular spectator sport, and an evening at the races is one of the quintessential Hong Kong things to do. Every Wednesday from September to June, the Happy Valley Racecourse comes alive with eight electrifying races and an accompanying carnival of food and wine. You can try your hand at betting, or simply enjoy the collective exhilaration, the smell of the turf and the thunder of ironed hoofs.

👁 Map p68, G5

跑馬地馬場

www.hkjc.com/english

2 Sports Rd, Happy Valley

admission $10

🕐 7-10.30pm Wed Sep-Jun

🚃 Happy Valley

Don't Miss

Placing a Bet

Pick up a betting slip and fill in four things: type of bet, race number, horse number(s) and amount of money you're betting (minimum is $10). Along with the cash, hand it to a staff member behind the betting windows at the back of the stands. You'll get a slip of paper, which you must show staff to claim your winnings after the race.

Betting Options

Here are some basic betting types:

▶ Win – you back one horse; it wins.

▶ Place – your horse finishes first, second or third.

▶ Quinella – you choose two horses; they come first and second, in either order.

▶ Quinella place – you back any two of the first three horses.

▶ Tierce – you choose the first three horses in correct order.

▶ Trio – like the tierce, but in any order.

Tours

To know more about horse racing, consider joining the 5½-hour **Come Horseracing Tour** (☏ reservations 2316 2151; per person $860), run during race meetings, which includes admission to the members' area, a buffet meal and a guided tour.

Racing Museum

Racing buffs can visit the **Hong Kong Racing Museum** (2nd fl, Happy Valley Stand; admission free; ☻10am-5pm Tue-Sun, to 12.30pm race days), which showcases celebrated trainers, jockeys and horseflesh.

☑ Top Tips

▶ Avoid crowds by leaving just before the last race. Walk 10 minutes to the Causeway Bay MTR station at Times Sq; turn right as you leave the turnstiles.

✗ Take a Break

There are high-price, decent-quality hot dogs and pizza at the racecourse. **Fiat Caffe** (www .fiat.com.hk; shop G5-G6, Leighton Centre, 77 Leighton Rd, Causeway Bay; ☻11am-10pm; Ⓜ Causeway Bay, exit A) offers excellent casual Italian fare served in small portions.

Local Life
Wan Chai Breather

Wan Chai is littered with hang-outs where residents or office workers go for a breather. These include not only parks, but unlikely havens where people can let off steam or space out before checking back into the world. To visitors, these eclectic spaces offer a different side of local society and some of the best food in town.

❶ Southern Playground

Seniors come to this **playground** (修頓遊樂場; ⏱6am-11.30pm; Ⓜ Wan Chai, exit A3) to play chess, and students to shoot hoops and kick ball. There are hip-hop dance-offs, housewives shaking a leg, outreach social workers, cruising gays and a trickle of lunchers. Wan Chai's social hub marks the boundary between home and play. It's said that in the 1950s, sailors visiting

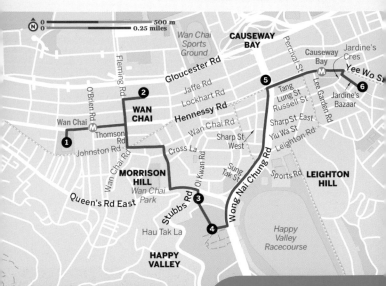

'Suzy Wong' bars ('hostess' bars that were popularised by the 1960 movie *The World of Suzy Wong* starring Nancy Kwan and William Holden) would never venture beyond this playground, no matter how drunk.

➋ Korean Lunch

A jealously guarded secret among foodies, **Joon Ko** (純子餐廳; 209 Jaffe Rd, Wan Chai; meals from $150; ⏾lunch & dinner; ⬧; Ⓜ Wan Chai, exit A1) serves authentic Korean dishes. Carnivores must try the beef ribs and ox tongue; while vegetarians shouldn't miss the cold noodles. The side dishes are equally well made, and what's more, generously refilled. Speak slowly when ordering; the Korean owners and the Nepalese staff understand little English.

➌ Khalsa Diwan Sikh Temple

In search of spirituality? This **temple** (www.khalsadiwan.com; 371 Queen's Rd E, Wan Chai; ⏾4am-9pm; 🚌), built in 1901, extends its services to any caste, colour or creed. Sunday prayer (9am to 1pm) sees 1000 believers and non-believers in worship; fewer at the daily prayers (4am to 8am, 6pm to 8pm). It also hands out free vegetarian meals (11.30am to 8.30pm).

➍ Hong Kong Cemetery

Nearby, opposite the racecourse, this crowded Protestant **cemetery** (香港墳場; Wong Nai Chung Rd; ⏾7am-6pm or 7pm; Ⓜ Causeway Bay, exit A) lies alongside Jewish, Hindu, Muslim and Catholic cemeteries. Tombstones date to the mid-1800s and include those of tycoons, colonialists and actresses. Given dead Hong Kong's parallels with the breathing city, an escapade here may prove quite enlightening.

➎ Rent-a-Curse Grannies

Under the Canal Rd flyover near Causeway Bay, you can pay rent-a-curse grannies to punch your enemy. For $50 these curse-muttering sorceresses will use a shoe to pound the hell out of a paper cut-out of anyone who vexes you. Villain exorcism (打小人, *da siu yan*) is believed to bring resolution.

➏ Japanese Dinner

Have dinner at cheerful **Iroha** (伊呂波燒肉; ☎2882 9877; www.iroha.com.hk; 2nd fl, 50 Jardine's Bazaar; lunch/dinner from $150/500; ⏾lunch & dinner; Ⓜ Causeway Bay, exit E) in Causeway Bay. It specialises in *yakiniku*, the Japanese style of grilling food over a burner. Among the dizzying range of Wagyu cuts on offer, the beef rib finger (*nakaochi karubi*) with its perfect fat-to-meat ratio and just-right chewiness comes highly recommended. If you love steak, be prepared to spend.

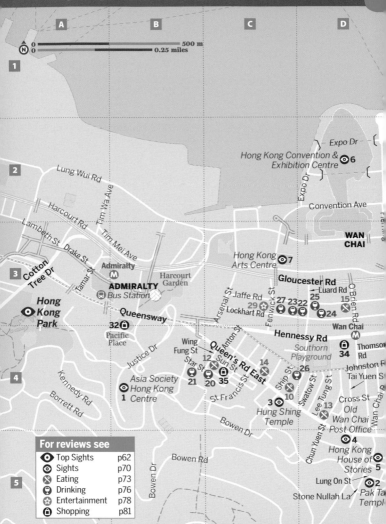

0 500 m
0 0.25 miles

Expo Dr

Hong Kong Convention & ⊙6
Exhibition Centre

Expo Dr

Convention Ave

WAN
CHAI

Lung Wui Rd

Harcourt Rd

Lambeth St   Drake St

Tim Wa Ave

Tim Mei Ave

Hong Kong ⊙7
Arts Centre

Gloucester Rd

Cotton
Tree Dr

Tamar St

Admiralty
Ⓜ

Harcourt
Garden

Luard Rd

Arsenal St

Jaffe Rd

Fenwick St

O'Brien Rd

27 23 22   25   15

Hong
Kong
Park ⊙

ADMIRALTY
Ⓑ Bus Station

Queensway

29   Lockhart Rd   24

Wan Chai
Ⓜ

32 Ⓐ

Pacific
Place

Justice Dr

Hennessy Rd

Southorn
Playground

34 Ⓐ   Thomson
Rd

Wing
Fung St

Queen's Rd East

Anton St

Sun St

14

Ship St

26

Johnston R

Tai Yuen S

Kennedy Rd

Asia Society
Hong Kong ⊙
1 Centre

Star St

21   20   35

St Francis St

Swatow St

Lee Tung St

10

3 ⊙

Cross St
Old
Wan Chai
Post Office

Borrett Rd

Hung Shing
Temple

13

Bowen Dr

Bowen Rd

Chun Yuen St

⊙4
Hong Kong
House of
Stories 5

Stone Nullah La

Lung On St

⊙2
Pak Ta
Templ

E **F** **G** **H**

VICTORIA
HARBOUR

Cross-
Harbour
Tunnel

Causeway Bay
Typhoon Shelter

1

Causeway
Bay

Kellett Island

Cargo
Handling
Basin

Wan Chai
Ferry Pier

Hung Hing Rd

8 Noonday
Gun

Victoria
Park

2

Houston St

36

9

Gloucester Rd

CAUSEWAY
BAY

Cannon St

Percival St

Jaffe Rd

Marsh St

Canal Rd

Lockhart Rd

28

18

Causeway
Bay

38

Great George St

Yee Wo St

3

Wan Chai
Sports
Ground

Tonnochy Rd

Harbour Rd

30

Harbour Dr

Stewart Rd

Marsh Rd

Jaffe Rd

Lockhart Rd

Hennessy Rd

Bowrington Rd

Tang Lung St

Russell St

Sharp St
East

Matheson St

Lee Garden Rd

Kai Chiu Rd

Jardine's Cres

Jun Ping Rd

Pennington St

Haven St

37

11

Foo Ming St

Hysan Ave

Leighton Rd

16

33

Yiu Wa St

19

Leighton Rd

Broadwood Link Rd

Caroline Hill Rd

CAROLINE
HILL

4

Wan Chai Rd

17

Yat Sin St

Cross La

Wood Rd

**MORRISON
HILL**

Oi Kwan Rd

Sports Rd

Wong Nai Chung Rd

**LEIGHTON
HILL**

Wan Cha
Park

Queen's Rd East

Stubbs

Hau Tak La

Wong Nai Chung Rd

Happy Valley
Racecourse

Ventris Rd

5

**HAPPY
VALLEY**

Sights

Asia Society Hong Kong Centre

GALLERY

1 Map p68, B4

Designed by architects Tod Williams and Billie Tsien, this magnificent site integrates 19th-century British military buildings, including two explosives magazines, and transforms them into an exhibition gallery, theatre, restaurant and bookstore. The horizontally oriented site offers an uplifting contrast to the skyscrapers nearby. It's an easy walk from Admiralty MTR station. (亞洲協會香港中心; The Hong Kong Jockey Club Former Explosives Magazine; ☑ 2103 9511; http://asiasociety.org/hong-kong; 9 Justice Dr, Admiralty; admission $10; ⊙gallery 11am-5pm Tue-Sun, to 8pm last Thu of month; Ⓜ Admiralty, exit F)

Take a Break Recharge with excellent and expensive tapas – but book ahead if going for lunch or dinner – at the centre's restaurant, **Ammo** (☑ 2537 9888; lunch set from $188, dinner from $400; ⊙11.30am-11.30pm Sun-Thu, to 12.30am Fri & Sat).

Pak Tai Temple

TEMPLE

2 Map p68, D5

This majestic Taoist temple was constructed 140 years ago by residents of Wan Chai, then a fishing village, to honour the god of the north because life-sustaining rivers flowed from the north. A 3m-tall statue of the deity (1604) sits in the main hall – long-haired, barefoot, with a creaseless face not the least perturbed by the ever-present threat of gentrification. (北帝廟; www.ctc.org.hk/en/directcontrol/temple10.asp; 2 Lung On St, Wan Chai; ⊙8am-5pm; Ⓜ Wan Chai, exit A3)

Take a Break Head to **Dalat** (大叻越南牛肉粉餐廳; Map p68, C4; ☑ 2527 6788; 10 Anton St; meals $40-90; ⊙11.30am-midnight; Ⓜ Admiralty, exit F) for cheap and cheery pho and curry with baguette.

Hung Shing Temple

TEMPLE

3 Map p68, C4

Originally a shrine overlooking the sea when the shoreline ran close to

Pak Tai Temple

its gates, tiny Hung Shing Temple (c 1847) still sits on a boulder, now staring at buildings and traffic. A red wooden staircase connects to the upper floor where a fortune teller runs his business. (洪聖廟; ☏2527 0804; www .ctc.org.hk/en/indirectcontrol/temple1.asp; 129-131 Queen's Rd E, Wan Chai; ⊙8am-5.30pm; Ⓜ Wan Chai, exit A3)

Old Wan Chai Post Office
HISTORIC BUILDING

4 ◎ Map p68, D5

A short distance east of Wan Chai Market is this tiny but important colonial-style building, erected in 1913 and now serving as an underwhelming resource centre operated by the Environmental Protection Department. (舊灣仔郵政

局; 221 Queen's Rd E, Wan Chai; ⊙10am-5pm Wed-Mon; Ⓠ6 or 6A)

Hong Kong House of Stories
MUSEUM

5 ◎ Map p68, D5

Opened by local residents, this tiny museum is located in the historic **Blue House**, a handsome pre-WWII building with cast-iron Spanish balconies reminiscent of New Orleans. Conservationists love it; those living in the area hate it. The not-for-profit museum runs tours in English; email one month ahead to arrange. (香港 故事館; ☏enquiries 2117 5850, tours 2835 4376; http://houseofstories.sjs.org.hk; 74 Stone Nullah Lane, Wan Chai; 2hr tour $600; ⊙11am-5pm; Ⓠ6 or 6A)

Hong Kong Convention & Exhibition Centre

BUILDING

6 ⊙ Map p68, D2

The massive Convention and Exhibition Centre, which was built in 1988 and extended onto an artificial island in the harbour for the official ceremony of the return of sovereignty to China in 1997, has been compared with a bird's wing, a banana leaf and a lotus petal. It's a leading venue in Asia for trade fairs and conventions. On the waterfront promenade just in front there's a 6m-tall statue of Hong Kong's symbol, called the Forever Blooming Bauhinia. The statue marks the return of Hong Kong to Chinese sovereignty and the establishment of the Hong Kong Special Administrative Region (SAR). (香港會議展覽中心; ☎2582 8888; www.hkcec.com.hk; 1 Expo Dr, Wan Chai; 🚌18)

Hong Kong Arts Centre

CULTURAL BUILDING

7 ⊙ Map p68, C3

Along with theatres and a bookshop, you'll also find at the HKAC the two-floor **Pao Sui Loong & Pao Yue Kong Galleries** (包玉剛及包兆龍畫廊 (包氏畫廊); admission free; ⊙10am-6pm, to 8pm during exhibitions), which hosts retrospectives and group shows in all visual media. (香港藝術中心; www.hkac.org.hk; 2 Harbour Rd, Wan Chai; Ⓜ Admiralty, exit E2)

Take a Break Stop at the centre's 4th-floor cafe, **Pumpernickel** (www.cafe pumpernickel.com; ⊙11am-9pm), for wholesome and affordable sandwiches, pastas and salads.

Noonday Gun

HISTORIC SITE

8 ⊙ Map p68, H2

Built in 1901, this recoil-mounted cannon, which is fired at noon every day, is one of the few vestiges of the colonial past in Causeway Bay. It's accessible via a tunnel through the basement car park in the World Trade Centre, just west of the Excelsior Hotel. From the taxi rank in front of the hotel, look west for the door marked 'Car Park Shroff, Marina Club & Noon Gun'. (香港怡和午炮; 221 Gloucester Rd; ⊙7am-midnight; Ⓜ Causeway Bay, exit D1)

Understand
Vickie's Angry Uncles

Victoria Park is associated with freedom of expression, due to the candlelight vigil that takes place on 4 June to commemorate the crackdown on democracy protests in China, and also due to the current-affairs debate 'City Forum' (noon to 1pm) that turns it into a mini Hyde Park every Sunday. During the show, a group of retired, pro-Communist old men – regulars of the park – will holler against speechifying prodemocracy politicians to drown them out. These men came to be known as the Uncles of Victoria Park (維園阿伯), but the term has since evolved to include any old man with a gripe.

Victoria Park

PARK

9 Map p68, H2

Victoria Park is the biggest patch of public greenery on Hong Kong Island. The best time to go is on a weekday morning, when it becomes a forest of people practising the slow-motion choreography of taichi. The park turns into a flower market a few days before the Chinese New Year. On Sunday, Indonesian domestic helpers gather here to pray, eat and socialise. (維多利亞公園; www.lcsd.gov.hk/en/ls_park.php; Causeway Rd; ☺6 or 7am-11pm; Ⓜ Tin Hau, exit B)

Take a Break Head to the classy **Dicken's Bar** (Map p68, H2; www.mandarin oriental.com/excelsior/dining/dickens_bar; basement, Excelsior Hong Kong, 281 Gloucester Rd; Ⓜ Causeway Bay, exit D1) for a rare ale and British pub grub.

Eating

Yin Yang

CHINESE $$$

10  Map p68, C4

Chef Margaret Xu grows organic vegetables and uses old-fashioned tools, such as stone-grinds and terracotta ovens, to create Hong Kong classics with a contemporary twist. Yin Yang is housed in a three-storey 1930s heritage building. Dinner is a tasting menu, but you'll have to book at least five days in advance, as it doesn't entertain walk-ins. (鴛鴦飯店; ☎2866 0868; www.yinyang.hk; 18 Ship St;

lunch $180-280, dinner from $680; ☺lunch & dinner Mon-Sat; Ⓜ Wan Chai, exit B2)

Ho Hung Kee

NOODLES $

11  Map p68, G3

The tasty noodles, wontons and congee at this bright little shop are cooked according to the ancient recipes of Ho's family, and clearly they still work. Ho Hung Kee has always been packed during lunch, even before it was awarded a Michelin star.

Yin Yang (p73)

(何洪記; ☑2577 6558; 2 Sharp St, Causeway Bay; meals $35-180; ⏰11.30am-11.30pm; Ⓜ Causeway Bay, exit A)

Cépage
MODERN FRENCH $$$

12 Map p68, C4

At this elegant address, the multi-talented chef, Sebastian Lepinoy, creates excellent French dishes that he presents like works of art. The menu includes classics such as pork belly, but magically transformed *sous vide* and topped with caviar. The wine list catalogues more than 2000 labels. (☑2861 3130; 23 Wing Fung St; lunch/dinner set from $370/680; ⏰lunch & dinner Mon-Sat; Ⓜ Admiralty, exit F)

Nino's Cozinha
PORTUGUESE, MACANESE $$

13 Map p68, D4

The Portuguese-Chinese couple here whip up solid Macanese and Portuguese classics that would give most restaurants in Macau a run for their money. Favourites such as the oxtail stew and baked duck rice evolved from heirloom recipes. Booking essential. (☑2866 1868; http://ninosgroup.com; 5th fl, 202 QRE Plaza, 202 Queen's Rd E, Wan Chai; meals $400-800; ⏰10am-11pm Tue-Sat, 11am-5pm Sun; Ⓜ Wan Chai, exit B2)

La Creperie
FRENCH $

14 Map p68, C4

Decorated like a quaint seaside town in Brittany, this is *the* go-to place for sumptuous galettes, airy crepes...and cider in a bowl. La Creperie is also one of the few places in town where you can have French andouille sausage. (☎2529 9280; 1st fl, 100 Queen's Rd E; meals from $100; ⏰11am-11pm; �止; Ⓜ Wan Chai, exit A3)

Mang Ambo's Filipino Restaurant
FILIPINO $

15 Map p68, D3

Pinoy domestic workers, musicians and businessmen come to this hole in the wall for its skewers, crispy pan-roasted pork and pork blood stew. A full meal will set you back a hefty $30. (☎2143 6877; 120 Jaffe Rd, Wan Chai; meals $25-40; ⏰11am-10pm; Ⓜ Wan Chai, exit A1)

Irori
JAPANESE $$

16 Map p68, G4

Irori's versatile kitchen turns out raw and cooked delicacies of an equally impressive standard. Seasonal fish is flown in regularly from Japan and carefully crafted into sushi and sashimi. To warm the stomach between cold dishes, there's a creative selection of tasty titbits, such as fried beef roll and yakitori (grilled skewers). (酒處; ☎2838 5939; 2nd fl, Dartlock Centre, Yiu Wa St, Causeway Bay; lunch/dinner from $150/300; ⏰lunch & dinner; Ⓜ Causeway Bay, exit A)

Old Bazaar Kitchen
ASIAN $

17 Map p68, F4

The short menu of tasty Singaporean, Malaysian and Chinese dishes at this unpretentious eatery is executed with such flair that food critics have been flocking here. Try the ox-tongue dishes and the noodles. (老巴刹廚房; ☎2893 3998; 207 Wan Chai Rd, Wan Chai; lunch/dinner from $50/150; ⏰lunch & dinner Mon-Sat; Ⓜ Wan Chai, exit A2)

Manor Seafood Restaurant
CANTONESE $$$

18 Map p68, G3

Upscale Manor does most Cantonese dishes and dim sum well, but is best known for its steamed crab and a now-rare classica. *Gum chin gai* (金錢雞, literally 'gold coin chicken') is a succulent cholesterol sandwich of chicken liver, barbecued pork and lard – all marinaded in Chinese wine, roasted to perfection and eaten between pancakes. It's guilt-laden, melt-in-your-mouth goodness. (富瑤酒家; ☎2836 9999; shop F-G, 440 Jaffe Rd, Causeway Bay; meals $300-2000; ⏰lunch & dinner; Ⓜ Causeway Bay, exit B)

IR 1968
INDONESIAN $$

19 Map p68, G4

Despite the year of its establishment (1968), this restaurant is all teak chic and Bali cool. It's rumoured that the handsome brothers manning the restaurant have almost as much pull as the beef *rendang* and the gado gado.

Understand
Chug Chug Ding A Ling

Nicknamed 'ding dings' by locals, trams have been sedately chugging back and forth between the Eastern and Western districts of the island since 1904. More than a century on, the world's largest fleet of double-decker tramcars – and Hong Kong's most low-carbon transport option – continues to negotiate pathways through the city's heavy traffic.

Board a 'ding ding' and watch the city unfold like a carousel of images as you relax and ponder tomorrow's itinerary. Viewing the districts east of Causeway Bay from a moving tram, moreover, imparts a cinematic quality that seeing these primarily residential districts on foot may not. Add speed to housing-block uniformity and you get rhythm and pattern. The district is served by around 30 stops on the eastbound tramline.

The bonus of riding on a tram is that you can hop off whenever something tickles your fancy. It's fun, too. High fives between passengers on passing vehicles are not unheard of.

There are lunch sets for $68 to $88. (印尼餐廳1968; ☎2577 9981; www.ir1968 .com; 28 Leighton Rd, Causeway Bay; meals from $180; ⏱noon-11pm; Ⓜ Causeway Bay, exit A)

Drinking

Classified Mozzarella Bar
BAR

20 Map p68, C4

We love the scrubbed wooden table, the designer lamp and the open frontage of this quiet and stylish bar. Take a seat near the footpath and people-watch as you enjoy your pick from 150 bottles and some quality tapas. (31 Wing Fung St, Wan Chai; Ⓜ Admiralty, exit F)

1/5 Nuevo
LOUNGE

21 Map p68, B4

The main draws of this sophisticated cocktail lounge with inviting leather and suede couches are the Spanish- and Latin American–inspired drinks made from fresh fruit, and the Cuban cigars. The tapas aren't too bad, either. It gets packed on the weekend with a dressy professional crowd, but it's still a good place to chill. (ground fl, 9 Star St, Wan Chai; ⏱2pm-2am Mon-Sat, from 5pm Sun, happy hr 5-9pm Mon-Sat; Ⓜ Admiralty, exit F)

Mes Amis
BAR

22 Map p68, D3

A slightly more stylish place in the lap of girly-club land, Mes Amis has a good range of wines and a Mediterranean-style snacks list.

There's a DJ from 11pm on Friday and Saturday. Mes Amis stays open till 6am on Friday and Saturday. (81-85 Lockhart Rd, Wan Chai; noon-2am Sun-Thu, to 6am Fri & Sat, happy hr 4-9pm; Ⓜ Wan Chai, exit C)

Amici
SPORTS BAR

23 Map p68, C3

The champion of Wan Chai sports bars features ample screens, five beers on tap, decent American-Italian food and a long happy hour. A few local football supporters' clubs have made Amici their base, and it's not hard to see why. The atmosphere during live broadcasts of big sporting events is contagious. (www.amicihk.com; 1st fl, Empire Land Commercial Centre, 81-85 Lockhart Rd, Wan Chai; noon-1am Sun-Thu, to 2am Fri & Sat, happy hr noon-9pm; Ⓜ Wan Chai, exit C)

Agave
BAR

24 Map p68, D3

Fans of tequila will be ecstatic here – there are 170 brands of the spirit, and the bartenders are heavy-handed with it. Interiors are brightly coloured, with cactus-themed adornments and a jovial atmosphere. Frisbee players like to hang out here. (shop C & D, 93 Lockhart Rd, Wan Chai; noon-1am, happy hr 3-9pm; Ⓜ Wan Chai, exit C)

Delaney's
BAR, PUB

25 Map p68, D3

At this popular Irish watering hole you can choose between the black-and-white-tiled pub on the ground

floor and a sports bar and restaurant on the 1st floor. The food is good and plentiful; the kitchen allegedly goes through 400kg of potatoes a week. (One Capital Place, 18 Luard Rd, Wan Chai; noon-2am, happy hr noon-9pm; Ⓜ Wan Chai, exit C)

The Pawn
PUB

26 Map p68, C4

This handsome three-storey establishment used to house tenement homes and a century-old pawn shop. Now it contains a restaurant and a bar. The slouchy sofas, shabby-chic interiors, and terrace spaces overlooking the tram tracks make it a pleasant location to sample the great selection of lagers, bitters and wine. (www.thepawn .com.hk; 62 Johnston Rd; 11am-2am Mon-Sat, to 11pm Sun; Ⓜ Wan Chai, exit A3)

Carnegie's
PUB

27 Map p68, C3

The rock memorabilia festooning the walls makes it all seem a bit Hard Rock Cafe-ish, but this place is worth a look, all the same. From 9pm on Friday and Saturday, Carnegie's fills up with young revellers, many of whom will end up dancing on the bar, which has brass railings in case they fall. (ground fl, 53-55 Lockhart Rd, Wan Chai; 11am-4am Mon-Thu, to 5am Fri & Sat, 5pm-4am Sun, happy hr 11am-9pm Mon-Sat; Ⓜ Wan Chai, exit C)

b.a.r. Executive Bar
LOUNGE

You won't be served if you just turn up at this clubby, masculine bar high above Causeway Bay (see **16** 🚇 Map p68, G4) – it's by appointment only. Odd, perhaps, but worth the trip if you're serious about whisky and bourbon. Several dozen varieties of whisky are served here, in large brandy balloons with large orbs of ice hand-chipped by the Japanese bartender. (📞2893 2080; 7th fl, Bartlock Centre, 3 Yiu Wa St, Causeway Bay; 🕑5pm-1am Mon-Sat; Ⓜ Causeway Bay, exit A)

Oriental Sake Bar Yu-Zen
LOUNGE

28 🚇 Map p68, G3

Sleek, with just a hint of decadence, this *sake* den offers a range of premium *sake* and creative cocktails. You can sip your drink sitting at the bar, or reclining like some modern opium smoker on cushions in a curtained dais. There's no happy hour. (http://hk-yuzen.com; 21st fl, Circle Plaza, 499 Hennessy Rd, Causeway Bay; cover charge $150; 🕑7pm-4am Mon-Sat, to 1am Sun; Ⓜ Causeway Bay, exit B2)

Entertainment

Hong Kong Arts Centre
CULTURAL VENUE

The Hong Kong Arts Centre (see **7** ◉ Map p68, C3) is a popular venue for dance, theatre and music performances. (香港藝術中心; 📞2582 0200; www.hkac.org.hk; 2 Harbour Rd, Wan Chai; Ⓜ Admiralty, exit E2)

Street Music Concert
LIVE MUSIC

Don't miss one of the free, outdoor gigs thrown by eclectic musician Kung Chi-sing. One Saturday a month, he puts on a concert outside the Hong Kong Arts Centre (see **7** ◉ Map p68, C3). The exciting line-ups have included anything from indie rock, punk and jazz to Cantonese opera and Mozart. It's excellent, professional-quality music performed in an electrifying atmosphere. Check website for dates. (📞2582 0280; www.hkac.org.hk; 🕑5.30-7.30pm one Sat a month)

LONELY PLANET/GETTY IMAGES ©

Hong Kong Convention & Exhibition Centre (p72)

Understand
Hong Kong Festivals

Hong Kong's calendar is with littered with colourful festivals celebrating Chinese culture and Western traditions, as well as art, film and music. To help you plan for your trip, here are some of the best events on the Hong Kong entertainment calendar:

Hong Kong Arts Festival (www.hk.artsfestival.org; ☺Feb-Mar) An extravaganza of music, drama and dance, featuring some of the world's top performers.

Hong Kong Sevens (www.hksevens.com, tickets www.hkrugby.com; ☺late Mar/early Apr) Rugby teams from all over the world come for three days of lightning-fast, 15-minute matches; a giant, international party.

Hong Kong International Film Festival (www.hkiff.org.hk; ☺Mar-Apr) Film buffs from mainland China and around Asia come to pay homage to Asia's top film festival.

Art Basel Hong Kong (http://hongkong.artbasel.com; ☺May) Local and international galleries come to Hong Kong's premier art fair, which takes place at the Hong Kong Convention and Exhibition Centre.

International Dragon Boat Races (www.hkdba.com.hk; ☺Jun or Jul) Hundreds of teams from the world over compete in Victoria Harbour.

Hong Kong Photo Festival (www.hkphotofest.org) An excellent biennial event that showcases the works of Hong Kong's photographers. Dates change; check the website.

Clockenflap Outdoor Music Festival (www.clockenflap.com; ☺Dec) This multi-act, outdoor indie event is the highlight in Hong Kong's live-music calendar.

Wanch

LIVE MUSIC

29 Map p68, C3

This place, which takes its name from what everyone calls the district, has live music (mostly rock and folk, with the occasional solo guitarist thrown in) seven nights a week from 9pm. Jam night is Monday from 8pm. When there's no live performance, the Wanch is a bit of a pick-up joint. (☎2861 1621; 54 Jaffe Rd, Wan Chai; Ⓜ Wan Chai, exit C)

Understand

Pollution in Hong Kong

Air Quality

Hong Kong's most pressing environmental problem is air pollution, responsible for up to 2000 premature deaths a year. Not surprisingly, it has become a highly charged political and economic issue. Mounting public pressure has forced the government to take more decisive measures in recent years to control emissions from vehicles and power plants, the major source of air pollution. Government statistics show that the emission of most air pollutants has gone down, except sulphur dioxide, thanks to increased coal-burning by power plants. That said, many travellers to Hong Kong might find it hard to breathe in congested areas such as Causeway Bay and Mong Kok.

If you have difficulty breathing on days when the official air pollution index is 'low', know it's not your lungs that are clouding your judgment, it's the 20-year-old yardstick (www.epd-asg.gov.hk) used by the Hong Kong government to measure the pollution. For a clearer picture, consult Greenpeace's Real Air Pollution Index (www.greenpeace.org/china/en/hk-airpollution-map), which follows the World Health Organization standard.

Waste

Three large landfills in the New Territories absorb all of Hong Kong's daily 16,500 tonnes of municipal waste (though they will soon be full). As space for building large landfills is limited, the government introduced waste reduction schemes in 1998, but progress has been slow. Only 40% of household waste is recycled.

Looking Ahead

The future of Hong Kong's environment will depend not only on the city's efforts, but also on whether pollution in the greater Pearl River Delta region is tamed. The most polluted water in Hong Kong is found in Deep Bay, which is shared with nearby Shenzhen, and Hong Kong's air quality deteriorates drastically when winds bring pollution from the north. The governments of Hong Kong and Guangdong are working together to tackle regional pollution. Though progress has been slow, their success will bring a greener Hong Kong and Pearl River Delta.

Punchline Comedy Club
COMEDY

30 ⭐ Map p68, E3

A veteran on the scene, the Punchline Comedy Club hosts local and imported acts every third Thursday, Friday and Saturday from 9pm to 11pm. Entry costs around $300. Book tickets online or call. (📞2598 1222; www.punchlinecomedy.com/hongkong; Duetto, 2nd fl, Sun Hung Kai Centre, 30 Harbour Rd, Wan Chai; 🚌18, alight at Wan Chai Sports Ground)

Shopping

Daydream Nation
CLOTHING

A 'Vogue Talent 2010' brand founded by two of the most creative local designers around – Kay Wong and her brother Jing, who's also a musician – DN is known for its highly wearable fashion and accessories that come with a touch of theatricality. Check its website for opening hours; it's in the Hong Kong Arts Centre (see 7 ◎ Map p68, C3). (📞3741 0758; www.daydream-nation.com; 2nd fl, Hong Kong Arts Centre, 2 Harbour Rd, Wan Chai; Ⓜ Admiralty, exit E2)

Eslite
BOOKS

31 🔒 Map p68, G3

Taiwan's famous Eslite bookstore has opened its first overseas branch in Hong Kong. Occupying three floors, it has plenty of space, friendly lighting and 100,000 titles (40% in non-Chinese languages). The night owls among the city's bookworms will dig it here. (誠品; 📞3419 6789; 8th-10th fl, Hysan Pl, 500 Hennessy Rd, Causeway Bay; 🕐 10am-11pm; Ⓜ Causeway Bay, exit F2)

Anteprima
CLOTHING

At Anteprima, in Pacific Place (see **32** 🔒 Map p68, B3), the sophisticated women's wear by a Milan-based Japanese designer comes with hefty price tags that belies its ethereality. That said, most of the pieces, in silk, wool and fine cotton, are made to outlast fashion fads. Bestsellers include the knitwear and signature 'wire bag'. (📞2918 0886; www.anteprima.com; shop 223, 2nd fl, Pacific Place, 88 Queensway, Admiralty; 🕐11am-8pm Sun-Thu, 11.30am-8.30pm Fri & Sat; Ⓜ Admiralty, exit F)

Pacific Place
MALL

32 🔒 Map p68, B3

Pacific Place has a couple of hundred outlets, dominated by higher-end men's and women's fashion and accessories. (太古廣場; 📞2844 8988; www.pacificplace.com.hk; 88 Queensway, Admiralty; Ⓜ Admiralty, exit F)

G.O.D.
HOMEWARES, GIFTS

33 🔒 Map p68, G4

If you only have time for one souvenir place, make it G.O.D.. This cheeky lifestyle store, named with an acronym that, they say, means 'goods of desire' and nothing else, gives a witty take on an older and less-affluent Hong Kong.

If you're into retro with a twist, you'll love it here. G.O.D. has five branches, including one at the Jockey Club Creative Arts Centre (JCCAC; p127). (www .god.com.hk; Leighton Centre, Sharp St E, Causeway Bay; M Causeway Bay, exit A)

Wan Chai Computer Centre
MALL

34 🔒 Map p68, D4

Between appointments, office workers pack themselves into this mall

---

Q Local Life
Wan Chai's Markets

The area sandwiched by Queen's Rd East and Johnston Rd in Wan Chai is a lively outdoor bazaar thronged with vendors, shoppers and parked cars. Cross St and the northern section of Stone Nullah Lane feature **wet markets** (Map p68, D4; ☺7.30am-7pm) in all their screaming splendour. **Tai Yuen Street** (太原街 (玩具街), *woon gui kaai*), aka 'toy street' to locals, has hawkers selling goldfish, plastic flowers and granny-style underwear, but it's best known for its traditional **toy shops** (Map p68, D4; 14-19 Tai Yuen St), where you'll find not only kiddies' playthings, but clockwork tin and other kidult collectibles. Spring Garden Lane and Wan Chai Rd are a treasure trove of shops selling everything from Indian and Southeast Asian spices to funerary offerings and gadgets.

---

right next to Southorn Playground, sometimes just so they can have their finger on the gadgetry pulse. It's got everything here from iPhones and tablets to notebooks, laptops and custom-made 'white box' computers. And air-con. There's some leeway for bargaining. (灣仔電腦城; 1st fl, Southorn Centre, 130-138 Hennessy Rd, Wan Chai; ☺10am-8pm Mon-Sat; M Wan Chai, exit B2)

Sonjia
CLOTHING, HOMEWARES

35 🔒 Map p68, C4

Anglo-Korean Hong Kong designer Sonjia Norman creates sumptuous women's wear in silk, velvet and cotton, much of it hand-finished with embroidery, in her atelier here. The adjoining store stocks a select bunch of homewares to suit every taste. (www.sonjiaonline.com; 2 Sun St, Wan Chai; ☺9.30am-7.30pm Mon-Sat; M Admiralty, exit F)

D-mop
CLOTHING, ACCESSORIES

36 🔒 Map p68, H2

Decked out in wood and steel, D-mop has a diverse selection, ranging from edgy dressy to chic street, and brands from all over the world. It's one of the sole retailers of Y-3 and Nike White Label. (www.d-mop.com.hk; 8 Kingston St, Causeway Bay; M Causeway Bay, exit E)

MICHAEL COYNE/GETTY IMAGES ©

Store display, Pacific Place mall (p81)

Yiu Fung Store FOOD

37 Map p68, G3

Hong Kong's most famous store (c 1960s) for Chinese pickles and preserved fruit features sour plum, liquorice-flavoured lemon, tangerine peel, pickled papaya and dried longan. Just before the Lunar New Year, it's crammed with shoppers. (么鳳; 3 Foo Ming St, Causeway Bay; Ⓜ Causeway Bay, exit A)

Island Beverley MALL

38 Map p68, H3

Crammed into buildings, up escalators and in back lanes are Hong Kong's malls of microshops selling local designer threads, garments from other parts of Asia and a kaleidoscope of kooky accessories. (金百利商場; 1 Great George St, Causeway Bay; Ⓜ Causeway Bay, exit D)

Explore

Hong Kong Island: Aberdeen & the South

This is Hong Kong Island's backyard playground – from the good beaches of Repulse Bay, Deep Water Bay and South Bay to shoppers' paradise Stanley Market and Horizon Plaza, and the excellent Ocean Park amusement park near Aberdeen, which packs in enough entertainment for a whole day.

The Sights in a Day

☀️ Do the half-hour **sampan tour** (p89) of the famous Aberdeen Typhoon Shelter, then head to **Horizon Plaza** (p93) in Ap Lei Chau for designer bargains. Spend one to two hours there and have lunch at **Tree Cafe** inside the plaza. Alternatively, you can spend all morning and most of the afternoon at **Ocean Park** (p89).

☀️ Bus it to Stanley and spend the rest of your afternoon suntanning and kayaking at **St Stephen's Beach** (p87), strolling along the waterfront, and checking out **Stanley Market** (p87) and **Murray House** (p87). If you're spending the morning at Ocean Park, depending on when you leave you can go to Stanley for a late-afternoon swim, and then have dinner at **Toby Inn** (p91).

🌙 Dine at **Spices** (p87) in Repulse Bay. For something even more special, bring your own food to secluded **South Bay** (p87) instead, for a picnic and a night swim with bioluminescent algae. (This works well for the Ocean Park option, too.)

 Local Life

Beach-Hopping on Island South (p86)

 Best of Hong Kong

Beaches

South Bay (p87)

Middle Bay (p87)

St Stephen's Beach (p87)

Eating

Ap Lei Chau Market Cooked Food Centre (p90)

Spices (p87)

Getting There

🚌 **Bus** Stanley, Repulse Bay & Deep Water Bay: buses 6A, 6X, 260 from below Exchange Sq (Central); buses 73, 973 from Aberdeen.

🚌 **Bus** Aberdeen: buses 73 and 973 from Stanley.

🚌 **Bus** Ap Lei Chau: bus 90 from Admiralty bus terminus; by commuter boat from Aberdeen Promenade.

Local Life
Beach-Hopping on Island South

Beach-hopping along the Island's southern coastline is fun and convenient. All beaches listed here have showers and changing facilities, and most have other sights and restaurants in the vicinity. In the summer, the waters around Stanley and Repulse Bay teem with bioluminescent algae. Go after sundown to swim with fireflies.

❶ Deep Water Bay

Start from the westernmost Deep Water Bay, a quiet little inlet with a beach flanked by shade trees. Though not as famous as its neighbour Repulse Bay, it's less crowded and its barbecue pits are a real draw for locals – a dip here, especially in late afternoon, is sometimes accompanied by the aromas of grilled meat.

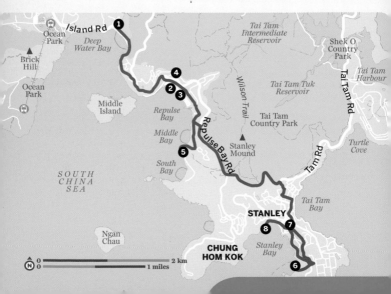

❷ Repulse Bay

From Deep Water Bay, take the scenic Seaview Promenade 2km to Repulse Bay, and be greeted by the sight of families and joggers going about their business. The long beach with tawny sand at Repulse Bay is packed almost all the time in summer. The water is murky, but it's good for people-watching.

❸ Around Repulse Bay

The hills here are strewn with luxury residences, including a wavy pastel building with a square hole in the middle, apparently a feature related to feng shui. At the beach's southeast end there's an assembly of deities and figures, as well as **Longevity Bridge** (長壽橋) – crossing the bridge is supposed to add three days to your life.

❹ Spices Restaurant

Spices (香辣軒; ☑ 2292 2821; www
.therepulsebay.com; The Repulse Bay, 109 Repulse Bay Rd; ☺ lunch & dinner Mon-Fri, lunch, tea & dinner Sat, Sun & public holidays), with its airy, colonial-style tropical interiors, is an ideal place for tea or a sundowner after a day at the beach. Sit on the terrace and enjoy palatable Asian selections such as curries and satays. Don't miss the homemade coconut ice cream!

❺ Middle Bay & South Bay

These attractive beaches are respectively 1km and 2km to the south of Repulse Bay. Middle Bay is popular with gay beachgoers, while French expats are drawn to South Bay. Swimming here on summer nights, you'll see specks of algae glowing like stars in the water.

❻ St Stephen's Beach

This hidden spot south of Stanley village is cleaner than Stanley Main Beach, and there are windsurfing boards and kayaks for hire. Take the bus to Stanley then walk south along Wong Ma Kok Rd. Turn right into Wong Ma Kok Path, then turn south and go past the boathouse to the beach.

❼ Stanley Village

The busy and labyrinthine **Stanley Market** (赤柱市集; ☺ 9am-6pm) has reasonably priced casual clothes (including large sizes and children's wear), linens, bric-a-brac and formulaic art.

❽ Murray House

Relocated from Central, **Murray House** (c 1844) is a three-storey classical building with breezy, wrap-around verandahs and a tiled roof with Chinese characteristics common in colonial architecture of that era.

Tai Tam Bay

Tam Rd

Tai Tam Rd

Stanley Bay

✕ 6

Carmel Rd

Tai Tam Reservoir

Tai Tam Intermediate Reservoir

Tai Tam Country Park

Wilson Trail

Stanley Mound (386m)

CHUNG HOM KOK

Violet Hill (433m)

Wong Nai Chung Reservoir

Repulse Bay Rd

Repulse Bay

Middle Bay

South Bay

✕ 8

Mt Nicholson (430m)

Aberdeen Tunnel

SHOUSON HILL

✕ 5

Island Rd

Deep Water Bay

Middle Island

Ngan Chau

SOUTH CHINA SEA

Aberdeen Country Park

Ocean Park

⊙ 1

Brick Hill

WONG CHUK HANG

Ocean Park

Aberdeen Lower Reservoir

Aberdeen Main Rd

✕ 7

Sham Wan

Aberdeen Channel

Ap Lei Pai

Peel Rise

ABERDEEN

Sampan Tours of Typhoon Shelter

Aberdeen Harbour

⊙ 3

✕ 4

AP LEI CHAU

9 ⋔

8th Estate Winery

2 ⊙

East Lamma Channel

2 km

1 miles

For reviews see

⊙ Sights	p89
✕ Eating	p90
⋔ Shopping	p93

Ⓝ

Sights

Ocean Park THEME PARK

1 ⊙ Map p88, C2

Hong Kong's home-grown theme park entertains with roller coasters, giant pandas, the world's largest aquarium (only 5000 fish!), and an atoll reef. The bifurcated complex is linked by a cable-car ride commanding terrific views of the South China Sea. (☑3923 2323; www.oceanpark.com.hk; Ocean Park Rd; adult/child 3-11yr $280/140; ⊙10am-7.30pm; 🚌6A, 6X, 70 & 75 from Central, 629 from Admiralty)

8th Estate Winery WINERY

2 ⊙ Map p88, A2

The world's only fully functional winery located inside an industrial building produces 100,000 bottles a year, with imported grapes aged in oak drums. Admission includes a tour and wine tasting; see website for times. Take bus 90 from Exchange Sq in Central, disembark at Ap Lei Chau bus terminus, then take a cab ($20). (☑2518 0922; www.the8estatewinery.com; Rm 306, 3rd fl, Harbour Industrial Ctr, 10 Lee Hing St, Ap Lei Chau; admission $100; ⊙usually 2-5pm most Sat & some Sun, by appointment Mon-Fri)

Understand
The Murray Puzzle

Murray House (see Local Life, p87) was relocated to Stanley in 2001 to make room for the Bank of China Building in Central. The Grade 1 heritage building was dismantled piece by piece, and all 4000 numbered pieces painstakingly reassembled at its new waterfront home. However, after the colossus was put back together again, six columns were left over. As you approach Murray House, you'll see the Ionic columns standing rather forlornly off to the left along the waterfront promenade. Note, too, some of the numbers still visible on the building blocks to the right of the entrance.

Sampan Tours of Typhoon Shelter TOUR

3 ⊙ Map p88, A2

Sampans will take you on a half-hour tour of the Aberdeen Typhoon Shelter (seen in *Lara Croft Tomb Raider: The Cradle of Life*) for about $70 per person. Embark from Aberdeen Promenade. Commuter boats also run between the Promenade and Ap Lei Chau ($1.80, five minutes).

Cable car to Ocean Park (p89), with views over Deep Water Bay

Eating

Ap Lei Chau Market Cooked Food Centre
CANTONESE $

4 Map p88, A2

The place to go for local flair and great seafood. Hawkers, including **Pak Kee** (☎2555 2984) and **Chu Kee** (☎2555 2052), cook for noisy dragon-boaters above a wet market. Order there or buy seafood from the market and have them cook it for you. Take minibus 36X from Lee Garden Rd in Causeway Bay, or a sampan from Aberdeen Promenade. (鴨利洲市政大廈; 1st fl, Ap Lei Chau Municipal Services Bldg, 8 Hung Shing St)

Crown Wine Cellars
EUROPEAN $$$

5 Map p88, C1

Wine connoisseurs and history fans will love this wine cellar, converted from a WWII ammo depot. You can tour the site and dine there by subscribing to a one-time membership. Take minibus 5 on Lockhart Rd, behind Sogo department store in Causeway Bay, and disembark at the top of Deep Water Bay Drive. (☎2580 6287; www.crownwinecellars.com; 18 Deep Water Bay Drive, Shouson Hill; meals from $400; ☺dinner Mon-Fri, lunch & dinner Sat & Sun)

Toby Inn

CANTONESE $

6 Map p88, E4

This modest eatery is Stanley's neighbourhood restaurant, with elders arriving for dim sum at the crack of dawn, hungry dragon-boaters dropping by for seafood after practice, and families coming in for simple dishes throughout the day. It's one of the few nontouristy eateries in Stanley. (赤柱酒家; ☏2813 2880; U1-U2, 126 Stanley Main St; meals $70-150; ⏰5.30am-10.30pm)

Jumbo Kingdom Floating Restaurant

CANTONESE $$

7 Map p88, B2

The larger of two floating restaurants, the Jumbo resembles the Imperial Palace crossbred with a casino (well, it is owned by a Macau casino mogul) – so kitsch that it's fun. That said, the dim sum and the Cantonese dishes are definitely authentic. If the interiors look familiar, it could be you've seen the film *Contagion* (2011) in which Gwyneth Paltrow attended a banquet here. Free transport to the restaurant is available from Aberdeen Promenade. (珍寶海鮮舫; ☏2553 9111; www.jumbo.com.hk; Sham Wan Pier Dr, Wong Chuk Hang; lunch $60-200; ⏰lunch & dinner Mon-Sat, breakfast, lunch & dinner Sun)

Verandah

INTERNATIONAL, ASIAN $$$

8 Map p88, D2

This beautiful replica of a colonial building has wooden ceiling fans, potted palms and a sea-facing

Understand
Hole in the Soul

Repulse Bay (see Local Life, p87) is surrounded by swanky high-rise apartment blocks. Among them is a giant pink, blue and yellow wavy structure with a giant square hole in the middle. Apparently this design feature was added on the advice of a feng shui expert. 'Chi', or energy flowing over mountains, is sometimes called a 'mountain dragon', and its course is called a 'dragon's vein'. Not all mountains have dragon's veins, but apparently this one does. And if it wasn't for the hole, the building would block the downward flow of this precious energy to the water, which would bring bad luck to the entire neighbourhood.

outlook; all lend a tropical feel. It's hushed and formal, with heavy white tablecloths and demurely clinking cutlery. The new marble staircase with wooden banisters will make professionals of the most inexperienced photographers. Verandah is famous for its afternoon tea, which is easily the south side's best. (露台餐廳; ☏2292 2822; www.therepulsebay.com; 1st fl, The Repulse Bay, 109 Repulse Bay Rd; ⏰lunch, tea & dinner Tue-Sat, brunch, tea & dinner Sun; 🚌6A, 6X)

Understand

Fishing Culture in Aberdeen

The main attraction of fishing port Aberdeen is the typhoon shelter (featured in the second *Lara Croft: Tomb Raider* movie) it shares with sleepy **Ap Lei Chau**, where the sampans of the boat-dwelling Tanka, a group that arrived in Hong Kong before the 10th century, used to be moored. Sometimes referred to as 'sea gypsies' by the British, the Tankas are believed to be descendants of certain ethnic minorities of southern China.

In 1961, the boat-dwelling population here stood at 28,000; now only a few hundred remain. While Lara Croft saw entire families going about their idyllic lives on a boat, you'll see motorised junks next to luxury yachts, and rusty shipyards alongside gleaming high-rises. In downtown Aberdeen, dry seafood stalls and mini-malls stand cheek by jowl.

People of the Water

The majority of inhabitants in Aberdeen and Ap Lei Chau are descendants of Tanka fishermen, who still see themselves as 'people of the water' (水上人; *sui seung yan*), and understand Tanka dialect. Each year this identity is flaunted with fanfare at dragon-boat races held throughout the territory. On weekday evenings, you may spot teams practising under the moon in the typhoon shelter, or chilling out in the Ap Lei Chau Market Cooked Food Centre (p90) after practice.

Dragon Boat

Hong Kong is the home of modern dragon-boat racing, an activity that originated 2000 years ago as a ritual for worshipping water deities. The city has the most teams (about 400) and the most races (over 20 per year) in the world, per square metre. It's a sport zealously embraced by all walks of life. Come racing season, even pasty-faced office workers will take up a paddle. The most spectacular events during the racing season (March to October) are the fishermen's races. You'll see junks moored in the harbour and decked out with flags, and people casting paper offerings into the water. The **Dragon Boat Association** (www.hkdba.com.hk) and **Hong Kong Tourist Board** (www.discoverhongkong.com) have listings of major events.

 Stanley Market (p87)

Shopping

Horizon Plaza FURNITURE, CLOTHING

9 🔒 Map p88, A2

The outlets in this enormous plaza sell furniture and off-season designer fashion (including the likes of Prada and Paul Smith) at reasonable prices. Most will ship, too. Get a directory from the lobby and start from the 28th floor. Bus 90 from Central's Exchange Sq terminus takes you to Ap Lei Chau Estate; from there take a cab. (新海怡廣場; 2 Lee Wing Street, Ap Lei Chau, Aberdeen; ⊙10am-7pm)

Take a Break The airy **Tree Cafe** (www.tree.com.hk/cafe; 28/F, Horizon Plaza; ⊙10.30am-7pm) offers solid sandwiches (from $45) and coffee.

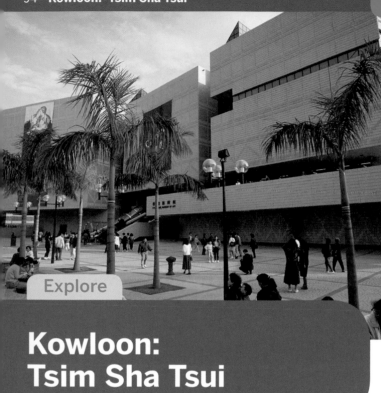

Explore

Kowloon: Tsim Sha Tsui

Tsim Sha Tsui, meaning 'sharp sandy point', is a vibrant district occupying the southern tip of the Kowloon Peninsula. Though best known for its shopping and dining, TST is also thick with museums and performance spaces. And with a population comprising Chinese, Indians, Filipinos, Nepalese, Africans and Europeans, it's Hong Kong's most cosmopolitan corner.

The Sights in a Day

 Spend an hour at the **Museum of History** (p99). Take a leisurely stroll to the Star Ferry Concourse via the scenic **Tsim Sha Tsui East Promenade** (p96), making small detours and stopping to check out sights along the way: **Middle Road Children's Playground** (p101), the **Hong Kong Museum of Art** (pictured left; p97), the **Clock Tower** (p97). That should take at least another two hours. Have an Indian vegetarian lunch at **Woodlands** (p105).

Spend two hours exploring Tsim Sha Tsui's unique heritage – the **Former Marine Police Headquarters** (p100), **Fook Tak Ancient Temple** (p99), **Kowloon Mosque** (p102), **St Andrew's Church** (p99), the **Former Kowloon British School** (p100) – ending with afternoon tea at the **Peninsula Hotel** (p101) or samosas and lassi at **Chungking Mansions** (p100) just opposite. Then head to the **Ocean Terminal** (p111) and/or **Rise Shopping Arcade** (p111) for some retail therapy.

Have dinner at **Dong Lai Shun** (p103) – consider ordering the mutton hotpot if it's cold out. Then head to Japanese-style **Butler** (p107) for fresh-fruit cocktails.

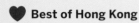

👁 Top Sights

Tsim Sha Tsui East Promenade (p96)

♥ Best of Hong Kong

Eating

Gaddi's (p104)

Ye Shanghai (p105)

Spring Deer (p105)

Museums

Hong Kong Museum of History (p99)

Hong Kong Museum of Art (p97)

Getting There

M MTR Tsim Sha Tsui and Jordan stations (Tsuen Wan line); East Tsim Sha Tsui station (West Rail line).

⚓ Star Ferry Western end of Salisbury Rd.

⚓ Macau Ferries The China Ferry Terminal is on Canton Rd.

Top Sights
Tsim Sha Tsui East Promenade

The resplendent views of Victoria Harbour make this walkway one of the best strolls in Hong Kong. Go during the day to take photos, visit the museums along the way and watch watercraft, families, lovers and tourists going about their business. After sundown, on your way to dinner or the Star Ferry, revisit the views, now magically transformed with the skyscrapers of Central and Wan Chai decked out in their neon robes.

◉ Map p98, C4

尖沙咀東部海濱花園

🚢 Star Ferry, Ⓜ Tsim Sha Tsui, exit J

Don't Miss

Clock Tower

The old Kowloon–Canton Railway Clock Tower (c 1915), in red brick and granite, is a landmark of the age of steam. The clocks began ticking on 22 March 1921 and haven't stopped since, except during the Japanese occupation.

Avenue of the Stars

Further north is Hong Kong's lacklustre tribute (星光大道) to its once-brilliant film industry. The highlight is a 2.5m-tall bronze statue of kung-fu icon Bruce Lee. From here, you can watch the **Symphony of Lights** (☉8-8.20pm), the world's largest permanent laser light show, projected from atop 40 skyscrapers.

Hong Kong Museum of Art

This excellent **museum** (香港藝術館; www.lcsd.gov.hk; 10 Salisbury Rd; adult/concession $10/5; free Wed; ☉10am-6pm Fri & Sun-Wed, to 8pm Sat) has seven galleries exhibiting Chinese antiquities and fine art, historical pictures and contemporary Hong Kong art; it also hosts temporary international exhibitions. Free English tours 11am Tuesday to Sunday.

Space Museum & Science Museum

The **Space Museum** (香港太空館; http://hk.space.museum; 10 Salisbury Rd; adult/child $10/5; free Wed; ☉1-9pm Mon & Wed-Fri, 10am-9pm Sat & Sun; Ⓜ East Tsim Sha Tsui, exit J) has 'sky shows', Omnimax films and a virtual paraglider. The giftshop sells dehydrated ice cream. Three storeys of action-packed displays at the **Science Museum** (香港科學館; http://hk.science.museum/eindex.php; 2 Science Museum Rd; adult/concession $25/12.50, free Wed; ☉1-9pm Mon-Wed & Fri, 10am-9pm Sat & Sun; Ⓜ Tsim Sha Tsui, exit B2) is a big attraction for youngsters.

☑ Top Tips

▶ Stairs near the Clock Tower lead to an elevated observation area.

▶ Stairs and a lift just past Avenue of the Stars lead to Tsim Sha Tsui East Podium Garden and Middle Rd Children's Playground.

✗ Take a Break

Deck N Beer (☉3-11pm Mon-Thu, to 1am Fri & Sat, 1-11pm Sun), at the Avenue of the Stars, has open frontage and decent beer. Hop inside the classy **InterContinental Lobby Lounge** (p108) for first-rate food and drinks.

TSIM SHA TSUI EAST

Science Museum Rd

Hong Kong Museum of History

1

Salisbury Rd

Tsim Sha Tsui East Ferry Pier

Granville Rd

Granville Sq

Cameron Rd

Mody Rd

13

22

East Tsim Sha Tsui (KCR East Rail Terminus)

17

Chatham Rd South

Observatory Rd

11 Granville St

Cct

37

31

Centenary Gardens

Hart Ave

Prat Ave

Mody Rd

16

Signal Hill Garden

24 Middle Road Children's Playground

28

26

Kimberley St

Kimberley Rd

HauFook St

32

Carnarvon Rd

Hanoi Rd

20 Minden Ave

Minden Row

St Andrew's Church

2

6

Knutsford Tce

Observatory Rd (Private)

Granville Rd

25 35

Cameron La

Cameron Rd

Humphreys Ave

Minden Ave

36

Chungking Mansions 4

19

Middle Rd

Middle Rd

Salisbury Rd

Salisbury Gardens

Former Kowloon British School

Chinese Garden

TSIM SHA TSUI

Kowloon Mosque & Islamic Centre

9

Nathan Rd

12

Tsim Sha Tsui

Lock Rd

33

Hankow Rd

39

Peking Rd

Peninsula Hotel

Hong Kong

8 27

Tsim Sha Tsui East

Aviary

Kowloon Park

10

Kowloon Park

Fook Tak Ancient Temple

34

14

Haiphong Rd

3

23

Kowloon Park Dr

15

21

Former Marine Police Headquarters

5

Tsim Sha Tsui East Promenade

29

Canton Rd

18

30

Star Ferry

HARBOUR CITY

China Ferry Terminal

VICTORIA HARBOUR

38

Star Ferry Bus Terminal

Star Ferry Terminal

500 m
0.25 miles

N

A B C D E

1 2 3 4

Sights

Hong Kong Museum of History
MUSEUM

1 Map p98, E1

The museum, one of Hong Kong's best, focuses on the territory's archaeology, natural history, ethnography and local history. There are splendid replicas of local traditions, such as ceremonial processions, old shops and streets. Don't miss the Hong Kong Story gallery. Free guided tours of the museum are available in English at 10.30am and 2.30pm on Saturday and Sunday. (香港歷史博物館; ☎2724 9042; http://hk .history.museum; 100 Chatham Rd S, Tsim Sha Tsui East; adult/child $10/5, free Wed; ☺10am-6pm Mon & Wed-Sat, to 7pm Sun; Ⓜ East Tsim Sha Tsui, exit P2)

Take a Break Have a yummy froyo at **Roll** (Map p98, D2; www.roll.hk; 41C-D Granville Rd; ☺11am-11pm), on the other side of Chatham Rd South.

St Andrew's Church
CHURCH

2 Map p98, C1

Hidden behind the Former Kowloon British School is Kowloon's oldest Protestant church. Built in 1905 in English Gothic style, it was turned into a Shinto shrine during the Japanese occupation. Nearby you'll see the former vicarage with its colonnaded balconies (c 1909). The church is accessed by steps or by a slope encircling a semi-circular space behind an old stone wall. (聖安德烈堂; www.standrews.org.hk; 138 Nathan Rd; ☺7.30am-10.30pm; Ⓜ Tsim Sha Tsui, exit B1)

Fook Tak Ancient Temple
TEMPLE

3 Map p98, B2

Tsim Sha Tsui's only temple is a smoky hole in the wall with a hot tin roof. Little is known about its ancestry except that it was a built in the Qing dynasty and renovated in 1900. Before WWII, worshippers of its Earth God were the coolies from nearby Kowloon Wharf, where the Ocean Terminal now stands. Today most incense offerers are white-haired octogenarians – the temple specialises in longevity. (福德古廟; 30 Haiphong Rd; ☺6am-8pm; Ⓜ Tsim Sha Tsui, exit C2)

Local Life
Learn Taichi for Free

Let a spritely master show you how to 'spread your wings like a stork' and 'wave hands like clouds' against the views of Victoria Harbour in front of the Hong Kong Museum of Art (p97). Taichi, or shadow boxing, is supposed to give you a sharper mind and a fitter heart. The lesson is offered free of charge by the Hong Kong Tourism Board, but preregistration is required. (☎2508 1234; www.discoverhongkong.com; Tsim Sha Tsui East Promenade; ☺8-9am Mon, Wed & Fri; Ⓜ Tsim Sha Tsui, exit J)

Take a Break **Tak Fat Beef Balls**
(德發牛肉丸; Map p98, B2; Haiphong Rd;
⏰9am-8pm) in Haiphong Rd Temporary Market next door, has cheap noodles with beef ball and Hong Kong–style milk tea.

Chungking Mansions
BUILDING

4 Map p98, C3

Everyone should come here once. Built in 1961, this ramshackle high-rise caters to all needs – from finding a bed and a curry lunch to changing Burmese kyat and getting a haircut. According to anthropologist Gordon Mathews, more than 120 different nationalities – predominantly south Asian and African – pass through its doors in a single year. Chungking has the best Indian grocery stores in town.

Top Tip
Hong Kong Museums Pass
The **Hong Kong Museums Pass** (admission 7 days $30, adult/senior & student 6 months $50/25, 1 yr $100/50) allows multiple entries to six of Hong Kong's museums: the Science Museum (p97), Hong Kong Museum of History (p99), Hong Kong Museum of Art (p97), Space Museum (p97; excluding the Space Theatre), Hong Kong Heritage Museum (p134) and Hong Kong Museum of Coastal Defence. It's available from any Hong Kong Tourism Board (HKTB) outlet and the participating museums.

(重慶大廈; 36-44 Nathan Rd; MTsim Sha Tsui, exit F)

Former Marine Police Headquarters
HISTORIC BUILDING

5 Map p98, B4

Built in 1884, this gorgeous Victorian complex is one of Hong Kong's oldest government buildings. In 2009 it was converted into a glamorous property called Heritage 1881. You can still see some of the old structures, such as stables, pigeon houses and a bomb shelter. Why 1881? The number '4' has a similar pronunciation to 'death' in Chinese, so the superstitious developer conveniently renumbered history to avoid bad business. (前水警總部; www.1881heritage.com; 2A Canton Rd; ⏰exhibition hall 10am-10pm; 🚢Star Ferry)

Former Kowloon British School
HISTORIC BUILDING

6 Map p98, C1

Hong Kong's oldest former school for expatriate children is an Edwardian building that now houses the **Antiquities and Monuments Office**, the official authority on the city's built heritage. Constructed in 1902, the school was subsequently modified to incorporate verandahs and high ceilings, prompted perhaps by the frequent fainting spells suffered by its delicate occupants. (前九龍英童學校; www.amo.gov.hk; 136 Nathan Rd; MTsim Sha Tsui, exit B1)

Afternoon tea at Peninsula Hotel Hong Kong

Middle Road Children's Playground

PARK

 7 Map p98, D3

This leafy playground, atop the East Tsim Sha Tsui MTR station, is usually quiet, but on weekends families and picnickers of as many ethnicities as there are ways to go down a slide, come here to enjoy themselves. Its eastern exit leads to the handsome **Tsim Sha Tsui East Waterfront Podium Garden** (尖沙咀東海濱平台花園) where you can linger over a book under white shade sails or make your way to the waterfront. (中間道兒童遊樂場; Middle Rd; ⏱7am-11pm; Ⓜ East Tsim Sha Tsui, exit K)

Take a Break Enjoy beer and German sausages at **King Ludwig Beer Hall** (p107), at the foot of the steps leading to the park.

Peninsula Hotel Hong Kong

HOTEL

8 Map p98, C3

Lording it over the southern tip of Kowloon, this grand dame of Asia evokes colonial elegance. Taking afternoon tea in the colonnaded lobby is one of the best experiences in town – dress neatly and be prepared to queue for a table. But it's well worth a look, even if you're not eating here. (香港半島酒店; ☎2920 2888; www.peninsula.com;

cnr Salisbury & Nathan Rds; M East Tsim Sha Tsui, exit L3)

Kowloon Mosque & Islamic Centre
MOSQUE

 Map p98, C2

Hong Kong's largest mosque occupies the site of a previous one built in 1896 for Muslim Indian troops garrisoned in barracks at Kowloon Park. The mosque, with its handsome dome, minarets and a carved marble exterior, accommodates 7000 worshippers. Non-Muslims should ask permission to enter. Remember to remove your shoes if you do. (九龍清真寺; ☎2724 0095; 105 Nathan Rd; ⏰5am-10pm; M Tsim Sha Tsui, exit A1)

Take a Break Unwind over reasonably priced meze and a shisha at **Ziafat** (p103).

Kowloon Park
PARK

 Map p98, B2

Built on the site of a barracks for Muslim Indian soldiers in the colonial army, Kowloon Park is an oasis of greenery and a refreshing escape from the hustle and bustle of Tsim Sha

---

Understand
TST, Breeze for the Feet

The crowds and the traffic might obscure it, but Tsim Sha Tsui is one of the most walkable urban areas in Hong Kong. Architect Freddie Hai once put a ruler on the area's footpaths and found most to be 250m to 300m in length. Metro stations have a catchment radius of 500m, the rough equivalent of an eight-minute stroll. At half the length, streets in TST take only four minutes to walk.

What's more, linking most of TST's meandering avenues are T-junctions (where one road joins another at right angles but does not cross it). The very layout of the T-junction creates a sense of neighbourly enclosure while dangling the promise of fresh horizons at every corner. So reaching Canton Rd from Peking Rd, would it be right to the Macau Ferry Terminal or left to the Space Museum? Compare this to the sprawling, criss-crossing grid that is Yau Ma Tei – a fascinating area buzzing with life, that could also alienate or disorient if you're new to it.

Good old Nathan Rd is never more than four blocks away, no matter where you're at in TST. Beginning just shy of the harbour, Kowloon's earliest strip of asphalt runs past Yau Ma Tei to end in Mong Kok, offering the reassurance of a linear narrative in a labyrinthine plot, and a choice of many, many endings.

Tsui. Pathways and walls criss-cross the grass, birds hop around in cages, and ancient Chinese banyans dot the landscape. (九龍公園; www.lcsd.gov.hk/parks/kp/en/index.php; 22 Austin Rd; ⏱6am-midnight; Ⓜ Tsim Sha Tsui, exit A1, Jordan, exit C1)

Eating

Chang Won Korean Restaurant
KOREAN $$

11 Map p98, D2

If you're looking for truly authentic Korean food, head for this place, just one of several restaurants along a stretch that makes up Tsim Sha Tsui's 'Little Korea'. You'll find many Korean eateries and minimarts along Kimberley St and Austin Ave, not too far away. (莊園韓國料理; ☎2368 4606; 1G Kimberley St; meals $160-300; ⏱noon-4am; Ⓜ Tsim Sha Tsui, exit B2)

Ziafat
MIDDLE EASTERN, INDIAN $

12 Map p98, C2

This halal restaurant serves up decent Middle Eastern and Indian fare, including falafel, kebabs and curries. You can come here to smoke shisha, too. It's located in an old building full of guesthouses, but the restaurant itself is clean, quiet and humbly furnished with Arabic art. (☎2312 1015; 6th fl, Harilela Mansion, 81 Nathan Rd; meals

$120-200; ⏱11am-midnight; ; Ⓜ Tsim Sha Tsui, exit R)

Dong Lai Shun
NORTHERN CHINESE $$

13 Map p98, E2

The Northern Chinese dishes here are superbly executed, and the Shanghainese, Sichuanese and Cantonese favourites are not far behind. Dong Lai Shun is famous for its mutton hotpot, which involves dunking paper-thin slices of mutton into boiling water and eating it with sesame sauce and other condiments. The atmosphere is a little formal, but the service is warm. (東來順; ☎2733 2020; www.rghk.com.hk; B2, The Royal Garden, 69 Mody Rd; lunch set $200-400, dinner set $300-450; ⏱lunch & dinner; ; Ⓜ East Tsim Sha Tsui, exit P2)

Carving Peking duck at Spring Deer

Din Tai Fung
SHANGHAINESE $

14 🍴 Map p98, B3

The dumplings, noodles and other Shanghainese classics at this famous Taiwanese chain can be anyone's comfort food. There's always a line at the door and it doesn't take reservations; it's best to go in the afternoon. (www.dintaifung.com.tw; shop 130, 3rd fl, 30 Canton Rd; ⏰11.30am-10.30pm; 🍴👶; Ⓜ Tsim Sha Tsui, exit C1)

Gaddi's
FRENCH $$$

Gaddi's, which opened just after WWII at the Peninsula Hotel (see 8 ◉ Map p98, C3), was for a long time a place where wealthy families celebrated special

occasions. Today the classical decor may be a tad stuffy, the live Filipino band gratuitous, but the food – traditional French with contemporary touches –is, without a doubt, still among the best in town. (📞2315 3171; www.peninsula.com/Hong_Kong; 1st fl, Peninsula Hotel, cnr Nathan & Salisbury Rds; lunch/dinner set from $450/1500; ⏰lunch & dinner; Ⓜ East Tsim Sha Tsui, exit L3)

T'ang Court
CANTONESE $$$

15 🍴 Map p98, B3

As befitting a restaurant named after China's greatest dynasty, T'ang Court has raised its speciality, Cantonese cooking, to an art. The atmosphere is plush and hushed, with deep-pile carpets and heavy silks, and the only noise you'll hear is yourself talking. If that seems too formal, rest assured, the service will make you feel right at home, like an emperor in his palace. (唐閣; ☎2375 1133; http://hongkong .langhamhotels.com; Langham Hotel, 8 Peking Rd; ⏰11am-2.30pm & 6-10.30pm Mon-Fri, noon-2.30pm & 6-10.30pm Sat & Sun; ✈♿; Ⓜ East Tsim Sha Tsui, exit L4)

Spring Deer NORTHERN CHINESE $

16 Map p98, D3

Hong Kong's most famous Peking duck is served here and the roast lamb is impressive, but the service can be about as welcoming as a Beijing winter, circa 1967. Spring Deer comes recommended by Michelin inspectors. Booking essential. (鹿鳴春; ☎2366 4012; 1st fl, 42 Mody Rd; meals $80-400; ⏰lunch & dinner; ✈; Ⓜ Tsim Sha Tsui, exit N2)

Woodlands INDIAN $

17 Map p98, D3

A favourite of Tsim Sha Tsui's Indian community, Woodlands comes highly recommended for its excellent South Indian fare and modest charm. Dithering gluttons should order the thali meal, a metal tray with samplings of curries, rice and dessert. (☎2369 3718; upper ground fl, 16 & 17 Wing On Plaza, 62 Mody Rd; meals $55-100; ⏰noon-3.30pm & 6.30-10.30pm; ✈; Ⓜ East Tsim Sha Tsui, exit P1)

Ye Shanghai SHANGHAINESE $$$

18 Map p98, B3

At 'Shanghai Nights', dark woods and subtle lighting, inspired by 1920s Shanghai, fill the air with romance. The modern culinary creations, which are lighter than traditional Shanghainese fare, are also exquisite. The only exceptions to the Shanghai-style harmony are the Cantonese dim sum served at lunch, though these are wonderful too. (夜上海; ☎2376 3322; www.elite-concepts.com; 6th fl, Marco Polo Hotel, Harbour City, Canton Rd; meals $300-600; ⏰ lunch & dinner; ✈♿; Ⓜ East Tsim Sha Tsui, exit L4)

Steak House STEAKHOUSE $$$

19 Map p98, D4

At this first-rate steakhouse, the imported beef exhilarates even without the trimmings (exotic salts and mustard blends, gourmet steak knives), and the salad bar ($300 per person) is a garden of delight. **Harbourside** (港畔餐廳; ☎2313 2495; ⏰6am-midnight), in the same hotel, has great pizzas, Western and Asian dishes and a Sunday champagne brunch (noon to 2.30pm) that's a favourite of the buffet brigade. (☎2313 2323; http://hongkong-ic .dining.intercontinental.com; InterContinental Hong Kong, 18 Salisbury Rd; meals from $400; ⏰6-11pm Mon-Sat, noon-2.30pm Sun; Ⓜ East Tsim Sha Tsui, exit J)

Understand

ABCs of Tao

During your stay in Hong Kong, you might see temples guarded by strongly coloured and fierce-looking gods. These are Taoist temples. Taoism is an indigenous Chinese religion originating in the shamanistic roots of Chinese civilisation. Though never declared a national religion, it thrived from the Tang to the Ming dynasties, and its influence has been ubiquitous in Chinese life. Unlike evangelical religions stressing crusading and personal conversion, Taoism addresses needs such as cures for illnesses, protection from evil spirits and funerary requirements. Unlike Buddhism, it does not attempt to sublimate the mundane.

Tao for the Road

In contemporary Hong Kong, construction projects, including those commissioned by the government and foreign-owned companies, are preceded by a ritual performed to appease the deities of nature, such as those ruling the earth. Offerings of fruit are piled on a makeshift shrine and incense sticks are lit. Similar rituals take place before the official shooting of a film or the opening of a new shop. It is believed that keeping the deities happy is important for health, safety and feng shui, the last a belief partly influenced by Taoism.

Tao for the Dead

The majority of funeral rites in Hong Kong are presided over by Taoist 'ritual specialists'. More colourful than Buddhist ceremonies, Taoist rites feature the continuous chanting of the scriptures to the rhythmic striking of *muyu* (a wooden, hand-held, slit drum), and elaborate procedures including the sprinkling of flowers on the ground to relieve bitterness.

Taoist Temples

During the first two weeks of the Lunar New Year, millions in Hong Kong pay their respects at Taoist temples. These tend to be more decorative than Buddhist places of worship, and there are no nuns or monks in the ones in Hong Kong, only the ritual specialists, who can marry and have children. Besides statues of mythical creatures in the temples, you'll see representations of the cypress (for friendship), the tortoise (for longevity), bamboo (for honour) and the bat (for divine blessing).

Drinking

Butler
BAR

20 Map p98, D3

A cocktail and whisky heaven hidden in the residential part of TST. You can flip the whisky magazines as you watch the bartender, Uchida, create his magical concoctions with the flair and precision of a master mixologist in Ginza. We loved the fruit cocktails made from fresh citruses. (5th fl, Mody House, 30 Mody Rd; cover charge $200; **M** East Tsim Sha Tsui, exit N2)

Aqua Spirit
BAR

21 Map p98, B3

This uberfashionable bar with two-storey, floor-to-ceiling windows commands dramatic views of the Hong Kong Island skyline. It's an awesome place for after-dinner drinks with a date. The tables by the windows have a cover charge of $2000 each. There's a DJ on weekends. (www.aqua.com.hk; 30th fl, 1 Peking Rd; ☺5pm-2am; **M** Tsim Sha Tsui, exit L5)

Tapas Bar
BAR

22 Map p98, E3

An intimate vibe and bistro-style decor make this a good place to unwind over champagne and tapas after a day of sightseeing. (www.shangri-la.com; lobby, Kowloon Shangri-La, 64 Mody Rd, Tsim Sha Tsui East; ☺3.30pm-1am; **M** East Tsim Sha Tsui, exit P1)

Ned Kelly's Last Stand
PUB

23 Map p98, B3

Named after a gun-toting Australian bushranger, Ned's is one of Hong Kong's oldest pubs. Most of the expats and tourists who come here are attracted by the laid-back atmosphere and the Dixieland jazz band that plays and cracks jokes between songs. The bar is filled with old posters, rugby jerseys and Oz-related paraphernalia. (☏2376 0562; 11A Ashley Rd; ☺11.30am-2am, happy hr 11.30am-9pm; **M** Tsim Sha Tsui, exit L5)

King Ludwig Beer Hall
BAR

24 Map p98, D4

This busy place, with antler lighting fixtures, is popular with visiting Germans and others hankering after pork knuckle, sauerkraut and German beer on tap, including Maisel's Weiss. It's located just under Middle Rd Children's Playground (p101). (☏2369 8328; www.kingparrot.com; 32 Salisbury Rd; ☺noon-1am Sun-Thu, to 2am Fri & Sat; **M** East Tsim Sha Tsui, exit J)

Vibes
LOUNGE

25 Map p98, C2

This pleasant al fresco bar comes with resident DJ, cabanas and random tropical greenery. Try its molecular cocktails, which involve liberal uses of liquid nitrogen and foam. (☏2315 5999; www.themirahotel.com; 5th fl, The Mira Hong Kong, 118 Nathan Rd; ☺3pm-midnight; **M** Tsim Sha Tsui, exit B1)

InterContinental Lobby Lounge
BAR

Soaring plate-glass and an unbeatable waterfront location (see 19 Map p98, D4) make this one of the best spots to soak up that Hong Kong Island skyline and take in the busy harbour, although you pay for the privilege. It's an ideal venue from which to watch the 8pm light show. (Hotel InterContinental Hong Kong, 18 Salisbury Rd; ⊙24hr; M East Tsim Sha Tsui, exit J)

Bahama Mama's
CLUB

26 ⊕ Map p98, D1

Bahama Mama's goes for a Caribbean-island feel, complete with palm trees and surfboards. It's a friendly spot

and on Friday and Saturday nights there's a DJ spinning and a young crowd (similar to that at Carnegie's in Wan Chai) out on the bonsai-sized dance floor. (4-5 Knutsford Tce; ⊙4pm-3am Mon-Thu, to 4am Fri & Sat, to 2am Sun, happy hr 5-9pm; M Tsim Sha Tsui, exit B1)

Felix
BAR

27 ⊕ Map p98, C3

Enjoy the fabulous view at this Philippe Starck–designed bar connected to Felix restaurant, one of the swankiest dining rooms in Hong Kong's poshest hotel. Guys, brace yourselves for a dramatic view through the gents' urinals. (☏2315 3188; 28th fl, Peninsula Hotel Hong Kong, cnr Salisbury & Nathan Rds; ⊙6pm-2am; M Tsim Sha Tsui, exit E)

Entertainment

Dada
LIVE MUSIC

28 ⭐ Map p98, D1

It may look a bit over the top (and naming yourself Dada is a convenient excuse for that), but this live-music venue is surprisingly relaxing, in an unconventional sort of way. Live 'jazz' Thursday, and R&B Friday and Saturday. (☏3763 8778; 2nd fl, Luxe Manor, 39 Kimberley Rd; ⊙11am-2am Mon-Sat, to 1am Sun; M Tsim Sha Tsui, exit X)

Top Tip

Learn Local Culture from Locals

One of the more interesting offerings from the **Hong Kong Tourism Board** (HKTB; ☏2508 1234; www .discoverhongkong.com) is a series of a dozen free cultural programs in English called Cultural Kaleidoscope. Run by local experts in their fields, topics covered include antiques, architecture, Cantonese opera, Chinese medicine, Chinese cake making, Chinese tea, diamonds, feng shui, kung fu, jade and pearl shopping and taichi.

Hong Kong Cultural Centre

CONCERT VENUE

29 ⭐ Map p98, B4

Clad in pink ceramic tiles and lacking a single window in one of the most dramatic spots in Hong Kong, this building's shell is an aesthetic stinker. However, inside you'll find a 2000-seat concert hall with a Rieger pipe organ and two theatres. It's home to the Hong Kong Philharmonic and the Hong Kong Chinese Orchestra, and major touring companies play here. (香港文化中心; ☎2734 2009; www.hk culturalcentre.gov.hk; 10 Salisbury Rd; tickets $100-500; Ⓜ Tsim Sha Tsui, exit E)

Shopping

Chinese Arts & Crafts

GIFTS & SOUVENIRS

30 🔒 Map p98, B4

From silk cushions to jade earrings, the pricey traditional-style gifts here show you can keep your head and your poise while swimming in tourist clichés. (中藝; ☎2735 4061; www.cachk .com; 1st fl, Star House, 3 Salisbury Rd; ⏰10am-9.30pm; Ⓜ Tsim Sha Tsui, exit L5)

Hong Kong Museum of Art (p97)

Top Tip
Worthwhile Fashion

Exorbitant rent has driven some of Hong Kong's most exciting fashion designers out of business or, like **Johanna Ho** (www.johannaho.com), to the internet. Johanna graduated from Central St Martin's, and designs chic casualwear for women. **Cocktail** (Map p98, B3; ☎ 3105 1090; shop B01A, Sun Arcade, 28 Canton Rd; Ⓜ Tsim Sha Tsui, exit A1) stocks a limited selection of her designs.

Initial
CLOTHING & ACCESSORIES

31 🔒 Map p98, D2

This attractive shop and cafe carries stylish, multifunctional urbanwear with European and Japanese influences. The clothes created by local designers are complemented by imported shoes, bags and costume jewellery. (☎ 2311 4223; www.initialfashion.com; shop 2, 48 Cameron Rd; ⏰ 11.30am-11.30pm; Ⓜ Tsim Sha Tsui, exit B2)

Granville Road Factory Outlets
CLOTHING & ACCESSORIES

32 🔒 Map p98, D2

If you have the time and inclination to rifle through racks and piles of factory seconds, the dozen-or-so factory outlets selling slightly premium mainstream casual and leisure brands along Granville Rd should reward you with costs a fraction of store price. (加連威老道出口店; Granville Rd; Ⓜ Tsim Sha Tsui, exit B2)

Curio Alley
GIFTS & SOUVENIRS

33 🔒 Map p98, C2

This is a fun place to shop for name chops, soapstone carvings, fans and other Chinese bric-a-brac. It's found in an alleyway between Lock and Hankow Rds, just south of Haiphong Rd. (⏰ 10am-8pm; Ⓜ Tsim Sha Tsui, exit C1)

I.T.
CLOTHING & ACCESSORIES

34 🔒 Map p98, B2

This trendy shop carries a snazzy selection of first-to-third-tier designer brands from Europe and Japan – similar to D-mop in Causeway Bay, but a little less edgy. Prices are high but not outrageous. The I.T. group has shops in all the major shopping areas. (www.ithk.com; shop LG01 & LG16-17, basement, Silvercord, 30 Canton Rd; Ⓜ Tsim Sha Tsui, exit A1)

David Chan Photo Shop
CAMERAS

35 🔒 Map p98, C2

If you've decided to give the digital age a miss altogether, or at least still use film cameras, this dealer is the most reputable used camera shop in town. The owner, David Chan, been working in the business since the 1960s, and has some pretty precious equipment in his collection. It's the place to buy expensive collectibles. (陳烘相機; ☎ 2723 3886; shop 15, ground fl, Champagne Court, 16 Kimberley Rd; ⏰ Mon-Sat; Ⓜ Tsim Sha Tsui, exit B1)

Premier Jewellery   JEWELLERY

36 🔒 Map p98, C3

This family business is directed by a qualified gemologist and is a firm favourite. If you're looking for something in particular, give it a day's notice to have a selection ready for you. It can also help you design your own piece. (愛寶珠寶; 📞 2368 0003; shop G14-15, ground fl, Holiday Inn Golden Mile Shopping Mall, 50 Nathan Rd; ⏰10am-7.30pm Mon-Sat, 10.30am-4pm Sun; Ⓜ Tsim Sha Tsui, exit G)

Rise Shopping Arcade   CLOTHING

37 🔒 Map p98, D2

Bursting the seams of this mini-mall is cheap streetwear from Hong Kong, Korea and Japan, with a few quasi-hip brands chucked in for good measure. Patience and a good eye could land you purchases fit for a *Vogue* photo shoot. (利時商場; 📞 2363 0301; www.rise-hk.com; 5-11 Granville Circuit; ⏰noon-9pm; Ⓜ Tsim Sha Tsui, exit B2)

Ocean Terminal   MALL

38 🔒 Map p98, A4

The building jutting 381m into the harbour is a cruise terminal and a shopping mall. Originally Kowloon Wharf Pier (c 1886), it was rebuilt and reopened in 1966 as the Ocean Terminal. Today it's part of the Harbour City shopping complex that stretches for 500m along Canton Rd. You enter it at the western end of the Clock Tower. (www.oceanterminal.com.hk; Salisbury Rd; ⏰10am-9pm; ⛴ Star Ferry)

Swindon Book Co Ltd   BOOKS

39 🔒 Map p98, C3

This is one of the best 'real' (as opposed to 'supermarket') bookshops. Its sister store is Central's Hong Kong Book Centre (p40). (辰衝; 📞 2366 8001; www.swindonbooks.com; 13-15 Lock Rd; ⏰9am-6.30pm Mon-Thu, to 7.30pm Fri & Sat, 12.30-6.30pm Sun; Ⓜ Tsim Sha Tsui, exit A1)

Explore

Kowloon: Yau Ma Tei & Mong Kok

Yau Ma Tei – meaning the place *(tei)* where fishermen waterproofed boats with oil *(yau)* and repaired hemp ropes *(ma)* – rewards the explorer with a close-up look at a more traditional Hong Kong. Congested Mong Kok (Prosperous Point) teems with shops selling electronics, clothes, shoes, jewellery and kitchen supplies, but a few cultural oases have also emerged in the area.

Sights in a Day

☀ Explore Yau Ma Tei's **Tin Hau Temple** (p117) and **Jade Market** (p117). Take a couple of hours to stroll the length of **Shanghai Street** (p117), poking your head into the shops, then have lunch at **Tim Ho Wan** (p121).

☼ Visit any combination of the following: **Ap Liu Street Flea Market** (p127), **Sik Sik Yuen Wong Tai Sin Temple** (p126), **Chi Lin Nunnery** (pictured left; p127), and speciality malls in **Mong Kok** (p123). Unwind at **Mido Cafe** (p121) in Yau Ma Tei.

☾ At 7pm, head to **Temple Street Night Market** (p114). Soak up the vibes and have dinner at **Hing Kee** (p120). At around 8.30pm, walk to **Yau Ma Tei Theatre** (p118) to look at the architecture. Then it's on to **Fullcup Café** (p122) in Mong Kok for drinks. If you're up to it, visit the century-old Yau Ma Tei **Wholesale Fruit Market** (p118) in the wee hours to see operations in full swing under the stars.

 Top Sights

Temple Street Night Market (p114)

♥ **Best of Hong Kong**

Shopping

Bruce Lee Club (p123)

Guitar Sofa (p125)

Yue Hwa Chinese Products Emporium (p124)

Mong Kok Computer Centre (p125)

Sin Tat Plaza (p124)

Markets

Temple Street Night Market (p114)

Wholesale Fruit Market (p118)

Getting There

Ⓜ **MTR** Jordan, Yau Ma Tei & Mong Kok stations (Tsuen Wan line).

🚌 **Bus** 2, 6, 6A and 9.

Top Sights
Temple Street Night Market

The liveliest night market in Hong Kong, Temple St extends from Man Ming Lane to Nanking St and is cut in two by Tin Hau temple. It's a great place to go for the bustling atmosphere, the aromas and tastes on offer from the food stalls, the occasional free Cantonese opera performance, and some shopping and fortune telling.

👁 Map p116, B4

廟街夜市

🕐 6-11pm

Ⓜ Yau Ma Tei, exit C

Don't Miss

Shopping

While you may find better bargains over the border in Shenzhen, it's more fun to shop here. The stalls are crammed with cheap clothes, watches, pirated CDs, fake labels, footwear, cookware, and everyday items. Any marked prices should be considered suggestions – this is definitely a place to bargain.

Street Food

For al fresco dining, head to Woo Sung St, which runs parallel to the east, or to the section of Temple St north of the temple. You can get anything from a bowl of noodles to Chiu Chow–style oyster omelettes and Nepalese curries, costing anywhere from $30 to $300. There are also quite a few seafood and hotpot restaurants in the area.

Fortune Telling

Every evening, a gaggle of fortune tellers sets up tents in the middle of the market; by reading your face, palm or date of birth, they'll make predictions about your life (consultations from $100). Some keep birds that have been trained to pick out 'fortune' cards. Questions of accuracy aside, it's all quite entertaining. Most of them speak some English.

Cantonese Opera

If you're in luck, you'll catch an extract of a Cantonese opera performed under the stars. Some of the most famous divas and maestros of the opera stage began their careers in this humble fashion (or so they say).

☑ Top Tips

▶ The market is at its best from 7pm to 10pm, when it's clogged with stalls and people.

✗ Take a Break

Mido Cafe (p121) has cheap local grub and a cool retro vibe. If it's full, head to nearby **Kubrick Bookstore & Cafe** (p123) for slightly pricier light bites and coffee.

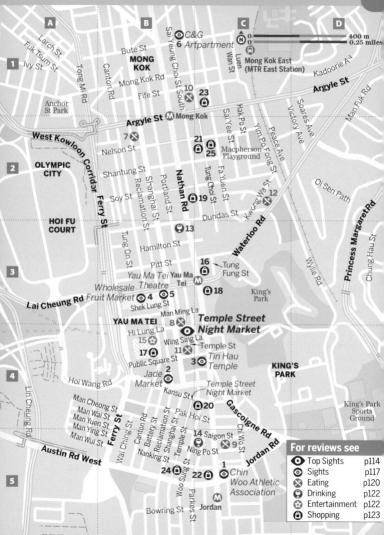

MONG KOK

Bute St

Canton Rd

Mong Kok Rd

Fife St

Sai Yeung Choi St South

C&G
Artpartment

Luen Wan St

Mong Kok East
(MTR East Station)

Kadoorie Av

Argyle St

Man Fuk Rd

Anchor
St Park

Argyle St Mong Kok

Hak Po St

Sai Yee St

Soares Ave

Victory Ave

Peace Ave

Yim Po Fong St

West Kowloon Corridor

Ferry St

Nelson St

OLYMPIC
CITY

Shantung St

Reclamation St

Shanghai St

Portland St

Soy St

Nathan Rd

Tung Choi St

Fa Yuen St

Macpherson
Playground

Oi Sen Path

HOI FU
COURT

Tung On St

Dundas St

Kwong Wa St

Waterloo Rd

Wylie Rd

Princess Margaret Rd

Chung Hau St

Hamilton St

Pitt St

Yau Ma Tei
Theatre

Yau Ma
Tei

Tung
Fung St

King's
Park

Lai Cheung Rd

Wholesale
Fruit Market

Shek Lung St

Man Ming La

Hi Lung La

Wing Sing La

Temple St

**Temple Street
Night Market**

**Tin Hau
Temple**

**KING'S
PARK**

Public Square St

Hoi Wang Rd

Jade
Market

Kansu St

Temple Street
Night Market

Gascoigne Rd

King's Park
Sports
Ground

Man Cheong St

Man Wai St

Man Yuen St

Man Ying St

Man Wui St

Ferry St

Wai Ching St

Canton Rd

Battery St

Reclamation St

Shanghai St

Temple St

Pak Hoi St

Saigon St

Ning Po St

Chi Wo St

Jordan Rd

Austin Rd West

Lin Cheung Rd

Woo Sung St

Parkes St

Bowring St

**Chin
Woo Athletic
Association**

Jordan

0 ____ 400 m
0 ____ 0.25 miles

For reviews see	
◉ Top Sights	p114
◉ Sights	p117
✖ Eating	p120
🍷 Drinking	p122
☆ Entertainment	p122
🛍 Shopping	p123

Sights

Chin Woo Athletic Association

HISTORIC SITE

1 Map p116, C5

This is an 88-year-old branch of the Chin Woo Athletic Association, founded 100 years ago in Shanghai by the famed kung-fu master Huo Yuanjia (霍元甲). The Shanghai Chin Woo was featured in Bruce Lee's *Fist of Fury* and Jet Li's *Fearless* in which Li played the master himself. There are classes that are open to overseas visitors but instructors teach mainly in Cantonese. You can visit the school during opening hours. (精武體育會; ☎2384 3238; Flat B & C, 13th fl, Wah Fung Bldg, 300 Nathan Rd, Yau Ma Tei; ☺2.30-9pm; Ⓜ Jordan, exit B1)

Jade Market

MARKET

2 Map p116, B4

Split into two parts by the loop formed by Battery St, this market has hundreds of stalls. The jade knick-knacks on sale here make great mementos and presents; unless you really know your nephrite from your jadeite, though, it's not wise to buy expensive pieces here. (玉器市場; Kansu & Battery Sts, Yau Ma Tei; ☺10am-6pm; Ⓜ Yau Ma Tei, exit C)

Local Life
Shanghai Street

Strolling down **Shanghai Street** (上海街; Map p116, B4; Ⓜ Yau Ma Tei, exit C) starting from Kansu St will take you back to a time long past. Once Kowloon's main drag, it's flanked by stores selling embroidered Chinese bridal gowns, sandalwood incense, kitchenware, Buddha statues, a pawn shop (at the corner of Saigon St), and mah-jong parlours (see the boxed text p122). It's a great place to shop for unusual souvenirs or a Buddhist home shrine if you ever need one. For a break, nip across Nathan Rd via an underground walkway for low-price, high-quality staples at Nathan Congee and Noodle (p120).

Tin Hau Temple

TEMPLE

3 Map p116, C4

This large, incense-filled sanctuary, built in the 19th century, is one of Hong Kong's most famous among temples dedicated to the goddess of the sea. The public square before it is Yau Ma Tei's communal heart, where fishermen once laid out their hemp ropes to dry in the sun next to Chinese banyans that today shade elderly chess players. (天后廟; cnr Public Square St & Nathan Rd, Yau Ma Tei; admission free; ☺8am-5pm; Ⓜ Yau Ma Tei, exit C)

STEVE VIDLER/CORBIS ©

Jade Market (p117)

Take a Break **Mido Cafe** (p121) has affordable Hong Kong–style drinks and snacks.

Wholesale Fruit Market
MARKET

4 ⊙ Map p116, B3

When the rest of the city is asleep, this listed historic market (built 1913) comes alive with wholesalers and vendors barking out prices, trucks offloading fresh fruit, and bare-backed workers manoeuvring mountains of boxes in front of two-storey brick-and-stone buildings featuring pre-WWII signboards. (油麻地果欄; cnr Shek Lung St & Reclamation Sts; ☯2-6am; Ⓜ Yau Ma Tei, exit D)

Yau Ma Tei Theatre
BUILDING

5 ⊙ Map p116, B3

Yau Ma Tei Theatre, with 1920s art-deco interiors, once kept many a rickshaw driver entertained with its blockbuster screenings, but after losing business to cinemas in the 1980s, it started showing erotic films to stay afloat. The neoclassical **'Red Brick House'** (紅磚屋) next door was the office of a pumping station (c 1895). The two historic buildings have since been converted into a Cantonese opera centre. (油麻地戲院; ✆enquiries 2264 8108, tickets 2374 2598; www.lcsd.gov.hk/ymtt; 6 Waterloo Rd; Ⓜ Yau Ma Tei, exit B2)

C&G Artpartment

GALLERY

6 ⊙ Map p116, B1

This exciting space behind the Pioneer Centre (始創中心) in Mong Kok is involved in nurturing the local art scene and representing socially-minded artists. The gallery has erratic opening hours, so call before you go. (☏2390 9332; www.candg-artpartment.com; 3rd fl, 222 Sai Yeung Choi St South, Mong Kok; ☺2-7.30pm Thu-Mon; Ⓜ Prince Edward, exit B2)

Understand
Hong Kong Occult

Feng Shui

Literally meaning 'wind water', feng shui (or geomancy) aims to balance the elements of nature to create a harmonious environment. It's been in practice since the 12th century, and it continues to influence the design of everything from high-rises to highways in Hong Kong. To guard against evil forces, which gain momentum when travelling in a straight line, doors are often positioned at an angle to each other. Ideally, homes and businesses should have a view of calm water – even a fish tank helps. Corporate executives shouldn't have offices that face west, otherwise their profits will go in the same direction as the setting sun.

Fortune Telling

A common method of divination in Hong Kong is the use of *chim* – the bamboo 'fortune sticks' found at temples. You shake a canister filled with these sticks until one falls to the ground. All the while, you contemplate a problem that's been bothering you. Each stick bears a numeral corresponding to lines of poetry printed on a slip of paper held by the temple guardian. You take the fallen stick to the temple guardian to redeem the piece of paper. You then ask the temple's fortune teller to interpret the poetic lines for you. Supposedly they're the answer to your problem.

Zodiac

The Chinese zodiac has 12 signs as does the Western one, but their representations are all animals. Your sign is based on the year of your birth (according to the Chinese lunar calendar). Being born or married in a particular year is believed to contribute to one's fortune. The year of the dragon sees the biggest jump in the birth rate, closely followed by the year of the tiger. Babies born in these years are believed to become noble and fearless leaders.

Top Tip

Upstairs Mong Kok

Mong Kok can be intense. After all, it is the most densely populated spot on the face of the earth. But you don't have to shun it. If you want to experience energetic MK without the insanity, make a beeline for its upstairs spaces. Above-the-ground oases include C&G Artpartment (p119), Fullcup Café (p122) and the Bruce Lee Club (p123). Sin Tat Plaza (p124) and Sino Centre (p123) are other options, but go during office hours to avoid crowds.

Eating

Ming Court
CANTONESE $$

7 Map p116, B2

At this classy hotel restaurant, laudable Cantonese cuisine is served in a bright dining room surrounded by replicas of ancient pottery. It's a good choice if you're looking for neat, modern surrounds in the midst of Mong Kok. Top-notch dim sum is available at lunchtime. (📞3552 3388; 6th fl, Langham Place Hotel, 555 Shanghai St, Mong Kok; lunch meals from $200, dinner meals from $350; Ⓜ Mong Kok, exit C3/E1)

Hing Kee Restaurant
DAI PAI DONG $

8 Map p116, B3

Hing Kee whips up hearty claypot rice and sumptuous oyster omelettes for families, night revellers and gangsters. (興記煲仔飯; 19 Temple St, Yau Ma Tei; meals from $30; ⏱5.30pm-1am; Ⓜ Yau Ma Tei, exit C)

Nathan Congee and Noodle
CONGEE, NOODLES $

9 Map p116, C5

This honest, low-key eatery has been making great congee and noodles for the last half-century. Order a side of fritters (to be dunked into the congee), tackle a rice dumpling or conquer the blanched fish skin. (彌敦粥麵家; 11 Saigon St, Yau Ma Tei; meals from $60; ⏱7.30am-11.30pm; Ⓜ Jordan, exit B2)

Good Hope Noodle
NOODLES $

10 Map p116, B1

Recommended by the Michelin guide, this busy noodle-stop is known far and wide for its terrific wonton soups and shredded pork noodles with spicy bean sauce. It's an eat-and-go sort of place, so don't come here if you feel like lingering. (好旺角麵家; 146 Sai Yeung Choi St South, Mong Kok; meals $25-80; ⏱11am-3am; Ⓜ Mong Kok, exit B3)

Mido Cafe

TEA CAFE **$**

11 Map p116, B4

This *cha chaan tang* (teahouse), a uniquely Hong Kong cafe with local dishes set in a 1950s building, serves meals throughout the day, but it's best to come at breakfast or in the afternoon for such oddities as *yin yang* (equal parts coffee and black tea with milk), *ling lok* (boiled cola with lemon and ginger) and Hong Kong–style French toast. (美都餐室; 63 Temple St, Yau Ma Tei; meals $25-80; ⏱7.30am-10pm; Ⓜ Yau Ma Tei, exit B2)

Tim Ho Wan

DIM SUM **$**

12 Map p116, C2

A former Four Seasons dim-sum chef recreates his magic in the world's first dim-sum eatery to receive a Michelin star. Get a ticket when you arrive, then go have a wander and check back in after half an hour, when a table should have become available. (添好運; ☑2332 2896; Shop 8, 2-20 Kwong Wa St, Mong Kok; meals $30-50; ⏱10am-9.15pm; Ⓜ Yau Ma Tei, exit 2A)

Dim sum treats

Understand
Badass Mah-Jong

On Shanghai St in Yau Ma Tei, you'll see **mah-jong parlours** (麻雀館) with signage showing '麻雀娛樂' ('mah-jong entertainment'). In the 1950s the four-player game of mah-jong was so popular that the British, despite their antigambling policy, began issuing licences to mah-jong parlours. There are now a few dozen parlours, down from 150 in their heyday. You may have seen them in Hong Kong–made gangster films as they were once associated with Triads, the Hong Kong mafia. Now with the police keeping a close eye, they're the civilised and noisy playgrounds of hardcore players. You can enter for a look, but remember that picture-taking is strictly forbidden.

Drinking

Fullcup Café
CAFE, LIVE MUSIC

13 🍸 Map p116, B3

'Full cup' sounds similar to the Chinese characters for 'breath', which is what this quirky, three-storey cafe offers – a breather in the midst of busy Mong Kok. Fullcup serves decent coffees, smoothies, beer and snacks; with an eclectic collection of retro furniture, it attracts a young, edgy crowd. There are live-music performances on most weekends. (呼吸咖啡茶館; 4-6th fl, Hanwai Commercial Centre, 36 Dundas St, Mong Kok; ⏰noon-3am; Ⓜ Yau Ma Tei, exit A1)

Snake King Yan
SPECIALITY SHOP

14 🍸 Map p116, C5

Challenge yourself to a shot of rice wine mixed with snake bile at this speciality shop near the Temple St Night Market (snake bile is believed to boost virility). If that repulses, there are also bottles of other exotic infusions on display that you might prefer. (蛇王恩; 80A Woo Sung St, Yau Ma Tei; ⏰noon-10pm; Ⓜ Jordan, exit A)

Entertainment

Broadway Cinematheque
CINEMA

15 ⭐ Map p116, B4

Yau Ma Tei may seem an unlikely place for an alternative cinema, but it's worth checking out for art-house new releases and reruns here. It's next to the Kubrick Bookstore & Cafe (p123). (百老匯電影中心; 📞2388 3188; www.cinema.com.hk; Prosperous Garden, 3 Public Square St, Yau Ma Tei; tickets $32-55; Ⓜ Yau Ma Tei, exit C)

Shopping

Bruce Lee Club
SOUVENIRS

16 🔒 Map p116, C3

Founded by Bruce Lee's fans, this mini-museum and souvenir shop has action figures, comic books, movie stills and posters, books and other memorabilia related to the kung-fu icon on display, some available for sale. It also hosts talks and demos several times a year, on the weekend. (李小龍會; ☎2771 7093; www.bruceleeclub.com; Shop 160-161, In's Point, 530 Nathan Rd; ⓘ1-9pm; Ⓜ Yau Ma Tei, exit A1)

Kubrick Bookstore & Cafe
BOOKS, COFFEE

17 🔒 Map p116, B4

This cafe and bookstore next to the Broadway Cinematheque (p122) has a great range of film-related books, magazines and paraphernalia, including a good selection in English. Kubrick also serves good coffee. (☎2384 5465; Shop H2, Prosperous Garden, 3 Public Square St, Yau Ma Tei; ⓘ11.30am-10pm; Ⓜ Yau Ma Tei, exit C)

Protrek
OUTDOOR EQUIPMENT

18 🔒 Map p116, C3

This reliable shop is arguably your best bet for outdoor gear that will see you through from summit to sea. The English-speaking staff are helpful. The shop also runs training courses for outdoor activities. (www.protrek.com.hk;

Getting Inked in Hong Kong

In the 1960s, sailors on shore leave in Hong Kong would go to dingy tattoo parlours in Tsim Sha Tsui to get inked with images of dragons or naked women. For anything else, you had to go abroad – until now.

Nic Tse, aka **South China Sea Collective** (南海合作社; Map p116, B1; ☎6333 5352; kowloonink@gmail.com; 2nd fl, 234 Sai Yeung Choi St South, Mong Kok; tattooing per hr $1000), belongs to a new generation of tattoo artists in Hong Kong who are well versed in tattoo styles of both Asian and Western cultures. Nic is Chinese, but speaks perfect English, and his repertoire includes realist armscapes to minimalist body art and everything in between. (But if you want a dragon, he can do that, too.) Interested parties should email Nic as early as possible to discuss details and book an appointment. Payment is in cash or via PayPal.

522 Nathan Rd, Yau Ma Tei; ⓘnoon-8pm Mon-Sat, 11.30am-9.30pm Sun; Ⓜ Yau Ma Tei, exit C)

Sino Centre
MALL

19 🔒 Map p116, B2

This shabby mall in the heart of Mong Kok is the go-to place for CDs (new and used), magazines, comics, action figures, computer games and other

Local Life
Chan Wah Kee Cutlery Store

At **Chan Wah Kee Cutlery Store** (陳華記刀莊; Map p116, B5; ☎2730 4091; 278D Temple St, Yau Ma Tei; ⏰11am-6pm, closed Wed; Ⓜ Jordan, exit C2) you can watch one of Asia's last remaining master knife-sharpeners in action. Eighty-year-old Mr Chan uses nine different stones to grind each blade, alternating between water and oil. His clients include chefs, butchers, tailors and domestic gourmands from all over the world. Customers have sent him their Japanese willow knives for his magic touch. Mr Chan charges between $100 and $600 to sharpen a blade, with a wait time of three months. However, if you buy a knife from him – there's a good selection – he'll sharpen it there and then. Prices range from $200 for a paring knife to $2000 for a Shun knife.

kidult bait. There are also fly-by-night bootleg DVD vendors. (信和中心; 582-592 Nathan Rd, Mong Kok; Ⓜ Yau Ma Tei, exit A2)

Tak Hing Dried Seafood
FOOD

20 🔒 Map p116, C4

This reliable corner establishment has glass jars stuffed with dried scallops, crocodile meat, edible bird's nest made from the salivary excretions of cave swifts, and oysters, though you might prefer their figs, cashews, candied lotus seeds and ginseng. (德興海味; 1 Woo Sung St, Yau Ma Tei; ⏰9am-7.30pm; Ⓜ Yau Ma Tei, exit C)

Tung Choi Street (Ladies') Market
MARKET

21 🔒 Map p116, C2

Also known as Ladies' Market (女人街), the Tung Choi St market is a cheek-by-jowl affair offering cheap clothes and trinkets. Vendors start setting up their stalls as early as noon, but it's best to get here between 1pm and 6pm, when there's much more on offer. (通菜街; Tung Choi St, Mong Kok; ⏰noon-10.30pm; Ⓜ Mong Kok, exit D3)

Yue Hwa Chinese Products Emporium
DEPARTMENT STORE

22 🔒 Map p116, C5

This cavernous place offers pretty much everything that a visiting souvenir hunter could ask for, with seven packed floors of ceramics, furniture, souvenirs and clothing, as well as bolts of silk, herbs, clothes, porcelain, luggage and kitchenware. (裕華國貨; www.yuehwa.com; 301-309 Nathan Rd, Yau Ma Tei; ⏰10am-10pm; Ⓜ Jordan, exit A)

Sin Tat Plaza
MALL

23 🔒 Map p116, C1

Sin Tat Plaza on busy Argyle St is *the* mall for iPhones, iPads, Android phones, Chinese-made replicas,

Tung Choi Street (Ladies') Market

knock-offs, parallel-import phones from Japan, Korea, the US and Europe – even phones that double as a lighter. You can also get your current phone unlocked here. Beware: it's also full of repackaged second-hand phones sold as new. (83 Argyle Street, Mong Kok; Ⓜ Mong Kok, exit D2)

Guitar Sofa
MUSICAL EQUIPMENT

24 🔒 Map p116, B5

This ubercool shop frequented by professional musicians has a consignment service for used electric and acoustic guitars and a variety of amplifiers. There are also new guitars for sale at very competitive prices. Check the website for the latest offerings.

(📞 2314 2122; www.guitarsofa.com; 10th fl, Lee Kong Commercial Bldg, 115 Woo Sung St, Yau Ma Tei; 🕐 11.30am-8.30pm Mon-Sat, to 7pm Sun; Ⓜ Jordan, exit A)

Mong Kok Computer Centre
MALL

25 🔒 Map p116, C2

Prices at this computer centre are cheap, with Chinese-made tablets selling for 50% to 70% of the price you'd pay for the same product in the US. They also custom-make 'white-boxes' (unbranded computers), but there are no computer parts for sale. Language can be a slight barrier for English speakers here. (8-8a Nelson St, Mong Kok; 🕐 1-10pm; Ⓜ Mong Kok, exit D3)

Top Sights
Sik Sik Yuen Wong Tai Sin Temple

Getting There

Ⓜ Wong Tai Sin, exit B2

A sensory whirl of roofs and pillars, intricate latticework, bridges, flowers and incense, this bustling Taoist temple, built in 1973, has something for all walks of Hong Kong society, from pensioners and tycoons to parents and young professionals. Some come simply to pray and thank the deity, some to divine their future, others to get hitched – Sik Sik Yuen is an appointed temple for Taoist weddings in Hong Kong.

Don't Miss

The Deity
Wong Tai Sin was a shepherd who was said to have transformed boulders into sheep. When he was 15, an immortal taught him how to make a potion that could cure all illnesses; he is thus worshipped by the sick and the health-conscious. The term 'Wong Tai Sin' is sometimes used to describe those who are generous to a fault.

Main Altar
The main altar is where ceremonies take place. The image of the deity was brought here from Guangdong province in 1915. Behind the main altar are the **Good Wish Gardens** (⏱9am-4pm; suggested donation $2), replete with pavilions and carp ponds.

Fortune Telling
To the left of the entrance is an arcade of fortune tellers (consultations from $100), some of whom speak English. You can also divine your future with *chim* – bamboo 'fortune sticks' that are shaken out of a box on to the ground and then interpreted by a fortune teller.

Nearby: Chi Lin Nunnery
Just one MTR stop away from the temple is this arresting Buddhist **nunnery** (志蓮淨苑; www.chilin .org; 5 Chi Lin Dr; admission free; ⏱9am-4.30pm nunnery, 6.30am-7pm garden; Ⓜ Diamond Hill, exit C2), rebuilt completely of wood in 1998 – with not a single nail – in the style of a Tang dynasty monastery.

Also in the complex is **Chi Lin Vegetarian** (龍門樓·志蓮素齋; Nan Lian Garden; meals from $150; ⏱11.30am-9pm; 🖉), an excellent restaurant.

嗇色園黃大仙祠

☑2327 8141, 2351 5640

www.siksikyuen.org.hk

2 Chuk Yuen Village, Wong Tai Sin

suggested donation $2

⏱7am-5.30pm

☑ Top Tips

▶ Colourful ceremonies take place in the main altar; call for times.

▶ Nearby: **Ap Liu Street Flea Market** (鴨寮街; Apliu St, btwn Nam Cheong & Yen Chow Sts, Sham Shui Po; ⏱noon-midnight; Ⓜ Sham Shui Po, exit A1): digital- and electronic-gadget heaven; **Jockey Club Creative Arts Centre** (賽馬會創意藝術中心; www.jccac.org.hk; 30 Pak Tin St, Shek Kip Mei; ⏱10am-10pm; Ⓜ Shek Kip Mei, exit C): former factory now artists' studios.

✗ Take a Break

Nearby **Wing Lai Yuen** (詠藜園四川菜館; 15-17 Fung Tak Rd; ⏱11am-11pm) has cheap and tasty Sichuanese noodles.

Explore

New Territories

Along with Lantau, the New Territories contain the rural and wild places of Hong Kong. Given the close proximity of seven million people, that might sound like an odd claim, but you really can get away from the city here. Extensive country parks, a world-class museum, interesting temples and a wetland centre are among the worthwhile attractions in this area.

The Sights in a Day

Get up early and head to Sai Kung with enough water and snacks to last three hours, then take a cab to the **High Island Reservoir East Dam** (p130) and begin hiking. Take lots of photos – it's one of Hong Kong's most beautiful places. Chat up the locals – Hong Kong's hikers are friendly people.

Walk back to Pak Tam Chung, then take a bus to Sai Kung. If you're tired and hungry, have tea at **Honeymoon Dessert** (p137), then make your way to Sha Tin to check out the **Hong Kong Heritage Museum** (p134) for a couple of hours. If you're feeling perky and there's enough time, go all the way to Yuen Long to see a magnificent walled village on the **Ping Shan Heritage Trail** (p135).

Have dinner at **Shatin 18** (p137) or at **Dah Wing Wah** (p137) in Yuen Long, depending on where you end up. Return to your hotel to shower. Then if you're still not ready for bed, head to Kowloon or the Island for drinks.

Local Life

Hiking in the New Territories (p130)

Best of Hong Kong

Temples

Tsing Shan Monastery (p135)

Activities

High Island Reservoir East Dam Trail (p130)

Lai Chi Wo – Bride's Pool (p131)

Tai Long Wan Trail (p131)

Getting There

🚇 **MTR** East and West Rail lines; Light Rail Transit (LRT) lines

🚌 **Bus Kowloon Motor Bus Co** (KMB; www.kmb.hk) and green minibuses fill gaps left by the MTR network

Local Life
Hiking in the New Territories

Some of Hong Kong's best hiking trails pass lofty peaks, wave-lapped coves, rustic hamlets, sprawling reserves and handsome reservoirs in the New Territories. Here are some picturesque routes favoured by locals; each is a suggestion for half a day's hike. For more, see www.hkwalkers .net. The Map Publications Centre (www.landsd.gov.hk/mapping/en/ pro&ser/products.htm) has maps detailing trails.

❶ High Island Reservoir East Dam Trail (萬宜水庫東壩遠足徑; **3-5 hours)**

Surreal and dramatic, High Island Reservoir East Dam (萬宜水庫東壩) has massive dolosse (anchor-shaped blocks), slanting volcanic columns and sapphire waters. Five-hour route: take bus 94 from Sai Kung town to Pak Tam Chung (北潭涌), walk to East Dam (9km, two hours via Tai Mong Tsai & Man Yee Rds), hike the

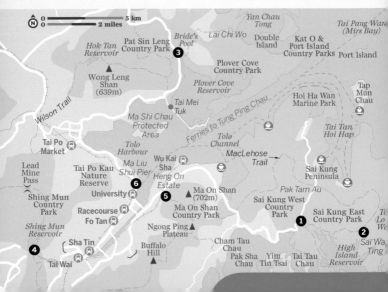

trail (1km, 30 minutes) then walk back. Three-hour route (advised): taxi from Sai Kung to East Dam ($130, 25 minutes), hike the trail and walk to Pak Tam Chung.

❷ Tai Long Wan Trail (大浪灣遠足徑; 4 hours)

This moderately challenging 12km trail passes delicious, swim-worthy bays (Sai Wan, Ham Tin, Chek Keng). Take bus 29R at Chan Man Rd (Sai Kung town), disembarking at the last stop, Sai Wan Ting (西灣亭); or take a taxi ($110). From the exit in Pak Tam Au (北潭凹), minibuses go back to Sai Kung.

❸ Bride's Pool – Lai Chi Wo (荔枝窩 – 新娘潭; 4½ hours)

This challenging 12km heritage and biodiversity trail passes mangrove forests and a huge Hakka village backed by an ancient 'feng shui' wood. Bride's Pool is a pool (潭) hemmed in by rocks below a waterfall. Route: Bride's Pool – Wu Kau Tang – Sam A Tsuen – Lai Chi Wo – Fan Shui Au – Bride's Pool Rd. At the bus terminus at Tai Po Market MTR station, catch bus 75K to Tai Mei Tuk (大美督) terminus, and from there, cab it to Bride's Pool ($80).

❹ Shing Mun Reservoir Trail (城門水塘遠足徑; 3 hours)

This easy 9.5km trail loops around Shing Mun Reservoir, passing a dappled country park and a valley with a gushing stream, into silent, almost magical, paper-bark forests. Take minibus 82 to Shiu Wo St (Tsuen Wan) and walk 20 minutes to Pineapple Dam (菠蘿壩). Go back the same way.

❺ Ma On Shan Country Park Trail (馬鞍山郊遊徑; 2½ hours)

This 4.5km trail runs past an old iron miners' settlement, up to the idyllic butterfly haven Ngong Ping Plateau (昂平), then to the villages of Tai Shui Tseng (大水井). Take bus 86K from Shatin MTR station, disembark at Heng On Estate roundabout and walk 45 minutes to the entrance. The exit is a short walk on Po Lo Che Rd to Sai Kung.

❻ Tung Ping Chau Walking Trail (東平洲步行徑; 2 hours)

This easy 6km hike around Hong Kong's deserted eastern island features eccentric rock layers, wave-beaten grottoes, lovely sea shards and waters teeming with corals and sea anemones. **Tsui Wah Ferry Services** (☏ 2272 2022; www.traway.com.hk; round trip $90) runs ferries here (Saturday, Sunday and public holidays) from Ma Liu Shui pier, near University station.

A   B   C   D

N 0 — 8 km
0 — 4 miles

SHENZHEN

1

Lok Ma Chau

3
Mai Po Marsh Nature Reserve

Lam Tseun North Country Park

2
Hong Kong Wetland Park

2

NEW TERRITORIES

Long Ping   Yuen Long

4
Tin Shui Wai   Ping Shan Heritage Trail
7

Kam Sheung Rd

3

Siu Hong

Tai Lam Country Park

Tai Mo Shan Country Park

Tsing Shan Monastery
6 Tuen Mun

MacLehose Trail

Tai Lam Chung Reservoir

Tai Lam Tunnel

4

Tsuen Wan West

Tsing Ma Bridge

Ma Wan

Kap Shui Mun Bridge

Tsing Yi

5

East Brother

West Brother

Lantau

E · F · G · H

1 · 2 · 3 · 4 · 5

Sheung Shui

Fanling

Pat Sin Leng Country Park

Hok Tan Reservoir

Pat Sin Leng Nature Trail

Wilson Trail

Wong Leng Shan (639m)

Plover Cove Country Park

Tolo Channel

Ma Shi Chau Protected Area

Tai Wo

Tai Po Market

Tolo Harbour

Ma On Shan

Wu Kai Sha

Heng On

Lead Mine Pass

Tai Mo Shan (957m)

Shing Mun Country Park

Tai Po Kau Nature Reserve

University

8 ✕

Tai Shui Hang

Ma On Shan (702m)

Sai Kung West Country Park

Racecourse

Fo Tan

Shek Mun

City One

Ma On Shan Country Park

Ngong Ping Plateau

5 ◉ Sai Kung

Shing Mun Tunnel

Sha Tin

Tai Wai

Sha Tin Wai

Buffalo Hill

Shing Mun Reservoir

1 ◉ Che Kung Temple

Hong Kong Heritage Museum

Lion Rock Country Park

Tate's Cairn Tunnel

Wilson Trail

Habe Haven

Kam Shan Country Park

Lion Rock Tunnel

Kowloon Tong

Kowloon Peak (602m)

YAU MA TEI

KWUN TONG

Sights

Hong Kong Heritage Museum

MUSEUM

1 ◎ Map p132, F4

This award-winning museum has magnificent displays on Cantonese opera and the cultural heritage of the New Territories, a fun Children's Discovery Gallery and, occasionally, the works of Hong Kong's photographers. (香港文化博物館; ☑2180 8188; www.heritagemuseum.gov.hk; 1 Man Lam Rd, Sha Tin; adult/concession $10/5, free Wed; ☺10am-6pm Mon & Wed-Sat, to 7pm Sun; ⓡChe Kung Temple)

Hong Kong Wetland Park

PARK

2 ◎ Map p132, B2

This wonderful 61-hectare park is located on one of the most important bird-migration routes in Asia, offering award-winning architecture and a fascinating look into wetland ecosystems. Take the West Rail line to Tin Shui Wai and board MTR Light Rail line 705 or 706. (香港濕地公園; ☑3152 2666, 2708 8885; www.wetlandpark.com; Wetland Park Rd, Tin Shui Wai; adult/child $30/15; ☺10am-5pm Wed-Mon; ⓡTin Shui Wai, light rail 705 or 706)

PAT BEHNKE/ALAMY ©

Hong Kong Heritage Museum

Mai Po Marsh Nature Reserve
WILDLIFE RESERVE

3 ◉ Map p132, C1

This 27-sq-km protected wetland is home to an amazing range of flora and fauna. There are three-hour English guided tours ($70; 9.30am, 10am, 2pm and 2.30pm Saturday, Sunday and public holidays). (米埔自然保護區; ☎2471 3480, www.wwf.org.hk; Sin Tin, Yuen Long; ⊙9am-5pm; ⏶Yuen Long, then ⏶76K)

Ping Shan Heritage Trail
VILLAGE

4 ◉ Map p132, B3

This 1km trail features buildings belonging to the Tang clan, including Hong Kong's oldest **pagoda**, a magnificent **ancestral hall** (⊙9am-1pm & 2-5pm), a temple and a **gallery** inside an old police station built by the British. Cross Tsui Sing Rd from the MTR station. (屏山文物徑; www.amo.gov.hk; Ping Shan Tsuen, Kam Tin, Yuen Long; ⊙10am-5pm Tue-Sun; ⏶Tin Shui Wai, exit E)

Sai Kung
NEIGHBOURHOOD

5 ◉ Map p132, H4

Most of the Sai Kung Peninsula is one huge 7500-hectare country park. Cosmopolitan Sai Kung town is where expats and visitors from the city like to hang out. (西貢; Ⓜ Choi Hung, then minibus 1A or 1M or ⏶92; ⏶Sha Tin, then ⏶299)

Understand
Victorian Roots

Hong Kong's two racecourses, Happy Valley Racecourse (p64) and Sha Tin Racecourse, are operated by the Hong Kong Jockey Club (HKJC). The HKJC is a recreation club that was started in the 19th century by Europeans who wanted to maintain their old lifestyle while living in Asia. They imported stallions from Mongolia and rode them themselves. The earliest races were annual affairs that any expat who was anyone at all would attend, including ladies. Nowadays weekly meetings are held at the racecourses.

Tsing Shan Monastery
TEMPLE

6 ◉ Map p132, A4

Hong Kong's oldest temple was founded 1500 years ago, and rebuilt in 1926. Some of the shrines and temples have slid into dilapidation; nonetheless they're imbued with a spooky charm. The temple appeared in Bruce Lee's *Enter the Dragon*. From the gates, it's a 30-minute walk to the monastery. (青山禪院; ☎2461 8050; Tsing Shan Monastery Path; ⊙24hr; ⏶light rail 610, 615, 615P to Tsing Shan Tsuen stop)

Understand

Early Hong Kong

- -

Hong Kong has supported human life since at least the Middle Neolithic Period (c 4000–2500 BC). Artefacts uncovered at almost 100 archaeological sites in the territory suggest the inhabitants of these settlements shared similar cultural characteristics as people living in the Pearl River Delta in China. The remnants of Bronze Age habitations (c 1500–220 BC) unearthed on Lamma and Lantau islands, and at around 20 other sites, also indicate that these early people practised some form of folk religion involving animal worship. Early Chinese historical records refer to the diverse maritime people in China's southeastern coastal area as the 'Hundred Yue' tribes. Some of the prehistoric inhabitants of Hong Kong might have belonged to these tribes.

The Five Great Clans

Hong Kong, along with the Yue tribes in Guangdong, was incorporated into the Chinese empire during the Qin dynasty (c 221–207 BC). Archaeological finds in the following centuries showed that Hong Kong came under the influence of Han culture as more Han settlers migrated to the region. The discovery of coins and pottery from Eastern Han dynasty (AD 25–220) on Lantau and Kau Sai Chau islands, and at several important digs, including a tomb at Lei Cheng Uk in central Kowloon and So Kwun Wat southeast of Tuen Mun, attests to this.

The first of Hong Kong's mighty 'Five Clans', Han Chinese, whose descendants hold political and economic clout to this day, began settling the area around the 11th century. The first and most powerful of the arrivals were the Tang, who initially settled around Kam Tin (*tin* means 'field'); see p135. The Tang were followed by the Hau and the Pang, who spread around present-day Sheung Shui and Fanling. These were followed by the Liu in the 14th century and the Man a century later.

Punti Versus Tanka

The Cantonese-speaking newcomers called themselves *bun-day* (Punti), meaning 'indigenous' or 'local' – something they clearly were not. They looked down on the original inhabitants, the Tanka, many of whom had been shunted off the land and had moved onto the sea to live on boats.

Eating

Chuen Kee Seafood Restaurant
CANTONESE $$

At Michelin-lauded Chuen Kee, in Sai Kung (see **5** Map p132, H4) you can pick your meal from the tanks of live seafood, agree on a price and they'll cook it for you the way you like. (全記海鮮菜館; ☎2792 6938; 87-89 Man Nin St, Sai Kung; ⏱7am-11pm; ⓧ; ⓡSha Tin, then 🚌299)

Dah Wing Wah
CANTONESE $

7 🍴 Map p132, B3

This famous oldie (c 1950) specialises in walled-village dishes such as lemon-steamed mullet and smoked oysters. Cantonese dim sum is served throughout the day. (大榮華酒樓; 2nd fl, Koon Wong Mansion, 2-6 On Ning Rd, Yuen Long; lunch/dinner from $120/200; ⏱6am-midnight; ⓡlight rail to Tai Tong Rd)

Shatin 18
NORTHERN CHINESE $$$

8 🍴 Map p132, G3

Lovely desserts and delectable views accompany Hong Kong's best Peking duck (24-hour advance booking required). (沙田18; ☎3723 1234; www.hong kong.shatin.hyatt.com; Hyatt Regency Hong Kong, 18 Chak Cheung St, Sha Tin; lunch/dinner from $300/400; ⏱ lunch & dinner; ⓧⓧ; ⓡUniversity)

Honeymoon Dessert
DESSERTS $

Branches in Asia, and 20 locations in town including this branch at Sai Kung (see **5** Map p132, H4), attest to Honeymoon's appeal. The sweet soups and fruit-based concoctions are indeed impressive. (滿記甜品; www.honeymoon-dessert.com; 9-10a, B&C Po Tung Rd, Sai Kung; dishes $30; ⏱1pm-2.45am; ⓧ; ⓡSha Tin, then 🚌299)

Top Sights
Tian Tan Buddha

Getting There

🚢 Outlying Islands Ferry Terminal, Central Pier 6 to Mui Wo, Lantau island

Ⓜ Tung Chung

🚌 Bus 2 from Mui Wo, bus 23 from Tung Chung

At 23m (10 storeys), Tian Tan Buddha on Ngong Ping Plateau, Lantau island, 500m above sea level, is the world's tallest seated bronze Buddha statue. In fact 'Big Buddha' is so big you can see it on the plane flying into Hong Kong, and, on a clear day, from Macau. Hikers negotiating the slopes of Lantau are often caught off-guard by 'Big Buddha' looming suddenly into view like an idea in a stark blue sky, or shrouded in fog like an afterthought.

Don't Miss

The Statue
Not many know this but the likeness of Lord Gautama was created by China Aerospace Science and Technology – the company that designs China's spaceships. The right hand is lifted in a gesture symbolic of a vow to eliminate suffering; the left is placed on the thigh, signifying compassion.

Exhibition Hall
The statue is reached by 268 steps. Inside the pedestal is an **exhibition hall** (☉10am-6pm) containing oil paintings and ceramic plaques of the Buddha's life and teachings. The large computer-operated bell chimes 108 times during the day to symbolise escape from the '108 vexations of mankind'.

Po Lin Monastery
Eclipsed by the new buildings in front is the century-old **Po Lin Monastery** (寶蓮寺; www.plm.org.hk; ☉9am-6pm), founded here by three monks from Jiangsu province in 1906. There are temples, a tea garden and a restaurant.

Ngong Ping 360
The most spectacular way to reach the plateau is by the 5.7km **Ngong Ping 360** (昂坪360; www.np360.com.hk; adult/child one way $86/44, return $125/62; ☉10am-6pm Mon-Fri, 9am-6.30pm Sat & Sun), a cable car linking Ngong Ping with Tung Chung downhill. The journey over the bay and the mountains takes 25 minutes in glassed-in gondolas.

天壇大佛

admission free

☉ 10am-6pm

☑ Top Tips

▶ Unless you like cheesy multimedia shows, skip Ngong Ping Village where the cable car stops uphill.

▶ **Mùtóu Guitar Workshop** (木頭結他工作室), where musician and prop designer **Wong Po-wah** (黃寶華; ☎9523 4916; wongpowah2005@yahoo.com.hk) handcrafts wooden electric guitars, is nearby in Mui Wo. Prices start from $15,000; it takes around three weeks, depending on specs. He ships too.

✕ Take a Break

Po Lin Vegetarian Restaurant (寶蓮禪寺齋堂; ☎2985 5248; Ngong Ping; meals $60-100; ☉11.30am-4.30pm; ☑) in the monastery offers cheap and filling vegetarian fare.

Decent, reasonably priced kebabs, noodles and desserts are at Ngong Ping Village.

Local Life
Lamma Island

Getting There

⚓ Outlying Islands Ferry Terminal, Central: Pier 4. Most sailings stop at the larger village Yung Shue Wan; some stop at Sok Kwu Wan.

Laidback Lamma attracts herb-growers, musicians and New Age therapists from a rainbow of cultures. Village stores stock Prosecco, and Chinese mongrels obey commands in French. Hike to the beach, your unlikely compass three coal-fired plants against the skyline, looking more trippy than grim. Spend the afternoon chilling, and in the evening glow, feast on prawns and calamari by the pier.

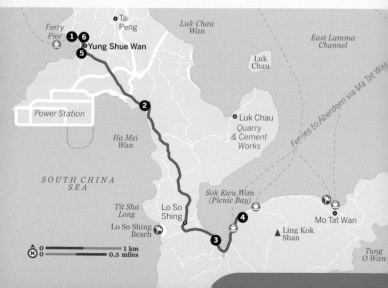

❶ Main Street, Yung Shue Wan

Spend a couple of hours exploring the shops in Yung Shue Wan (Banyan Bay). There's a small **Tin Hau temple** (c late 19th century) at the street's southern end. Stop for 'shepherdess' pie at ecoconscious **Bookworm Cafe** (南島書蟲; bookwormcafe.com.hk; 79 Main St, Yung Shue Wan; ⏰10am-9pm Mon-Fri, 9am-10pm Sat, 9am-9pm Sun; 🍴@), which doubles as a secondhand bookshop.

❷ Hung Shing Yeh Beach

All fuelled up, begin the hour-long (4km) Family Trail that runs between Yung Shue Wan and Sok Kwu Wan. Lamma's most popular beach, Hung Shing Yeh, is located midway along the trail, and on weekdays it's almost deserted. There are changing rooms, but you may want to pack your own picnic.

❸ Kamikaze Caves

Before entering Sok Kwu Wan, you'll pass three 'kamikaze caves': grottoes measuring 10m wide and 30m deep and built by the occupying Japanese forces to house motorboats wired with explosives to disrupt Allied shipping during WWII. They were never used.

❹ Sok Kwu Wan

At idyllic Sok Kwu Wan (Picnic Bay, but literally 'strings and fishnets bay'), there's **Lamma Fisherfolk's Village** (漁民文化村; lammafisherfolks.com.hk; adult/child $60/$50; ⏰10am-7pm Mon-Fri), a floating museum and theme park that showcases Hong Kong's fishing culture, and a renovated **Tin Hau temple** (天后廟), c 1826.

❺ Lamcombe Seafood Restaurant

Hike back to Yung Shue Wan for dinner. **Lamcombe** (南江海鮮酒樓; ☎2982 0881; 47 Main St, Yung Shue Wan; meals from $150; ⏰lunch & dinner) has been serving up tasty fried squid and steamed scallops for over 10 years. Portions are big and service is decent.

❻ Island Society Bar

Need one for the road? This **bar** (南島會; 6 Main St, Yung Shue Wan; ⏰5pm-late Mon-Fri, noon-late Sat & Sun) is the closest one to the ferry pier and the oldest watering hole on Lamma. Long-term expats come here for the low-down on everything. It's also the home of the feisty Lamma ladies' dragon-boat team.

Explore

Trip to Macau

China's Special Administrative Region (SAR) of Macau may be known as the Vegas of the East, but the city has much more to offer than casinos. There are fortresses, churches and neighbourhoods that evoke the style of its former Portuguese masters, intermixed with Chinese temples and shrines. And of course, no trip to Macau is complete without tasting Macanese food, a delicious celebration of hybridism.

The Sights in a Day

☀ Spend 90 minutes at the **Ruins of the Church of St Paul** (p144) and the **Macau Museum** (p151) above it. Wander southwest through the tiny streets towards the Inner Harbour, stopping at the **Mandarin's House** (p151) and **St Joseph's Seminary Church** (p145). Have an early lunch at **Alfonso III** (p153), then cab it north to the lovely **St Lazarus Church District** (p153) to browse the boutiques and art spaces for a while.

☀ Head up to **Guia Fort** (p150) for a visit to the tiny but gorgeous Chapel of Our Lady of Guia. Don't miss the lighthouse and the panoramic views of the city. Then, if you like, spend an hour or so checking out one of the city's many casinos.

☾ Have dinner at **A Petisqueira** (p153) in Taipa. Make your way back to Macau Peninsula for drinks and live music at **Macau Soul** (p154).

 Top Sights

Ruins of the Church of St Paul (p144)

Local Life

Exploring Taipa & Coloane Islands (p146)

♥ **Best of Macau**

Eating
Antonio (p154)

Drinking
Macallan Whisky Bar & Lounge (p154)

Getting There

⛴ **Ferry** Catch the **TurboJet** (⌕790 7039, in Hong Kong 852-2859 3333 information, 852-2921 6688 bookings; www .turbojet.com.hk; HK$142-275) from the **Hong Kong–Macau Ferry Terminal** (200 Connaught Rd, Sheung Wan) or the slightly slower **New World First Ferry** (⌕2872 7676, in Hong Kong 852-2131 8181; www.nwff.com.hk; HK$140-275) from the **China Ferry Terminal** (33 Canton Rd, Tsim Sha Tsui). Both trips take about an hour.

Top Sights
Ruins of the Church of St Paul

Essentially a magnificent gate to nowhere, the ruins of the Church of St Paul are Macau's most treasured icon. Once part of a Jesuit church, it was designed by an Italian and built by exiled Japanese Christians and Chinese craftsmen in 1602. However, due to a fire in 1835, all that remains is its weathered facade and majestic stairway. Yet with its surviving statues, portals and engravings – what has been called a 'sermon in stone' – some still consider it to be the greatest monument to Christianity in Asia.

⦿ Map p148, B2

大三巴牌坊; Ruinas de Igreja de São Paulo

Travessa de São Paulo

admission free

⦿24hr

🚌 8A, 17, 26 (disembark at Luis de Camoes Garden)

Don't Miss

Asian Details

Though Christian in appearance, the facade is full of Asian details. On the third tier stands the Virgin Mary being assumed into heaven along with two flowers: the peony, representing China, and the chrysanthemum, a symbol of Japan. Look for Chinese lion gargoyles and, just beneath the pediment, a dragon surmounted by the Holy Virgin.

Stairway

The facade is approached by six flights of 11 stairs each, divided by landings with an elegant balustrade running up each side. The stairs are decentred to the left because there once were buildings in place of the floral display now running the length of the stairs on the right.

Museum of Sacred Art

This small **museum** (天主教藝術博物館; Museu de Arte Sacra; Rua de São Paulo; admission free; ⊙9am-6pm) contains polychrome carved wooden statues, silver chalices and oil paintings. The adjoining **crypt** (墓室; Museu de Arte Sacra e Cripta; admission free; ⊙9am-6pm) holds the remains of martyrs.

Nearby: Churches

With a scalloped entrance canopy (European), a roof of beams and rafters (Chinese) and China's oldest dome, **St Joseph's Seminary Church** (聖若瑟修院及聖堂; Capela do Seminario São Jose; Rua do Seminario; ⊙10am-5pm; ☐9, 16), built 1746 to 1758, is Macau's best example of tropicalised baroque architecture. The 17th-century baroque **Church of St Dominic** (玫瑰聖母堂; Igreja de São Domingos; Largo de São Domingos; ⊙8am-6pm; ☐3,6) has a fine altar and ecclesiastical art in its treasury.

☑ **Top Tips**

▶ To beat the crowds, get to the facade before 9am, then visit the museum as soon as it opens.

✖ **Take a Break**

Recharge with decent tapas at **Corner Wine Bar & Tapas Café** (p154), or head to **Macau Soul** (p154) for drinks and snacks.

Local Life
Exploring Taipa & Coloane Islands

Taipa was created from two islands joined together by silt from the Pearl River. Land reclamation has succeeded in doing the same thing to Taipa and Coloane, now joined by the Cotai Strip, 'Cotai' being a portmanteau of Coloane and Taipa. Scenic Taipa has rapidly urbanised, though you'll still find old shops alongside delicious Macanese eateries. The small island of Coloane was once a haven for pirates but today largely retains Macau's old way of life.

① Taipa Village
Take bus 22, 26 or 33 to get to this village in the south of the island, where the historical part of Taipa is best preserved. With a tidy sprawl of traditional Chinese shops and some excellent restaurants, the village is punctuated by grand colonial villas,

churches and ancient temples. Avenida da Praia, a tree-lined esplanade with wrought-iron benches, is perfect for a leisurely stroll.

❷ Museum of Taipa & Coloane History

This **museum** (路氹歷史館; Museu da História da Taipa e Coloane; Rua Correia da Silva; adult/student & senior MOP$5/2, free Tue; ⏱10am-6pm Tue-Sun) in the village has a display of excavated relics and other artefacts on the 1st floor, while the 2nd floor contains religious objects, handicrafts and architectural models.

❸ Pak Tai Temple

Sitting quietly in a leafy square in the village is this **temple** (北帝廟; Templo Pak Tai; Rua do Regedor), built in 1844 and dedicated to the Taoist god of the north. A pair of Chinese lions guards the entrance to the temple.

❹ Taipa House Museum

Further afield, the pastel-toned **villas** (龍環葡韻住宅式博物館; Casa Museum da Taipa; Avenida da Praia; adult/student MOP$5/3, free Tue; ⏱10am-6pm Tue-Sun) here were once the summer residences of middle-class Macanese; now they're museums showcasing Portuguese traditions, Macau's traditional industries and local life in the early 20th century.

❺ Chapel of St Francis Xavier

Head to Coloane by bus 21A from the bus stop on Estrada Governador Nobre de Carvalho, and alight at Coloane Village. The highlight here is this quirky **chapel** (聖方濟各教堂; Capela de São Francisco Xavier; Avenida de Cinco de Outubro; ⏱10am-8pm), built in 1928, which contains paintings of the infant Christ with a Chinese Madonna, as well as other interesting artefacts of Christianity and colonialism in Asia.

❻ Temples

Southeast of the chapel is quaint **Kun Iam Temple** (觀音廟; btwn Travessa de Caetano & Travessa de Pagode; ⏱10am-4pm Mon-Fri, to 1pm Sat). A little further to the southeast, there's a **Tin Hau Temple** (天后廟) on Avenida da Republica up in Largo Tin Hau Miu. At the south end of Avenida de Cinco de Outubro, Taoist **Tam Kong Temple** (譚公廟; ⏱8.30am-6pm) has a model of a dragon boat made from whalebone.

1 km
0.5 miles

SOUTH
CHINA
SEA

Av Norte da Amizade

Ponte da Amizade
Friendship Bridge

Rua dos Pescadores

Reservoir

Cemetery

AFA (Art for All
3 Society)

Estrada da
Areia Preta

Av do Nordeste

Av do Coronel
Mesquita

Montanha
Russa
Garden

5 Pavilion

Av do, Mong Ha Multi-sport

Fisherman's
Wharf

2 Macau
Museum
of Art

Avenida Xian Xing Hái

Avenida da Amizade

Av de Luís Gonzaga Gomes

Guia
Hill

Av do Conselheiro
Ferreira de Almeida

Kun Iam
Temple

Av Horta e Costa

Lou
Lim Ioc
Garden

Estrada do
Cemitério

Guia Fort
4

Macau
Peninsula

Rua de Luís Gonzaga Rodrigues

Rua de Paris

NAPE

Av de Lisboa

Av Dr Sun Yat Sen

Rotunda
de Carlos
da Maia

6 Monte Fort
& Macau
Museum

8 St Lazarus
Church District

Largo de São

Rua de St Xing Hái

São Domingos

Avenida de Dr Rodrigo Rodrigues

St Francis
Garden

Avenida do Dr Rodrigo Rodrigues

15 Jardim
de Artes

Ponte Governador
Nobre de Carvalho

Luís de
Camões Garden
& Grotto

Rua da Ribeira do Patane

Inner
Harbour

**Ruins of
the Church
of St Paul**

Travessa de São
Paulo

Seminário

Largo do Senado

Rua do Almirante Sérgio

Rua de Almeida Ribeiro

New
Yaohan Site

Rua Central

9

Rua de St
Agostinho

Mandarin's
House 7

Rua da Largo
Barra do Lilau

10

Penha
Hill

Baía da Praia
(Lagos de
Nam Van)

Avenida Doutor Stanley Ho

Av Dr Sun
Yat Sen

Lago
Sai Van

Av da R República

A-Ma
Temple 1

Rua de São
Tiago da Barra

Qianshan
Waterway

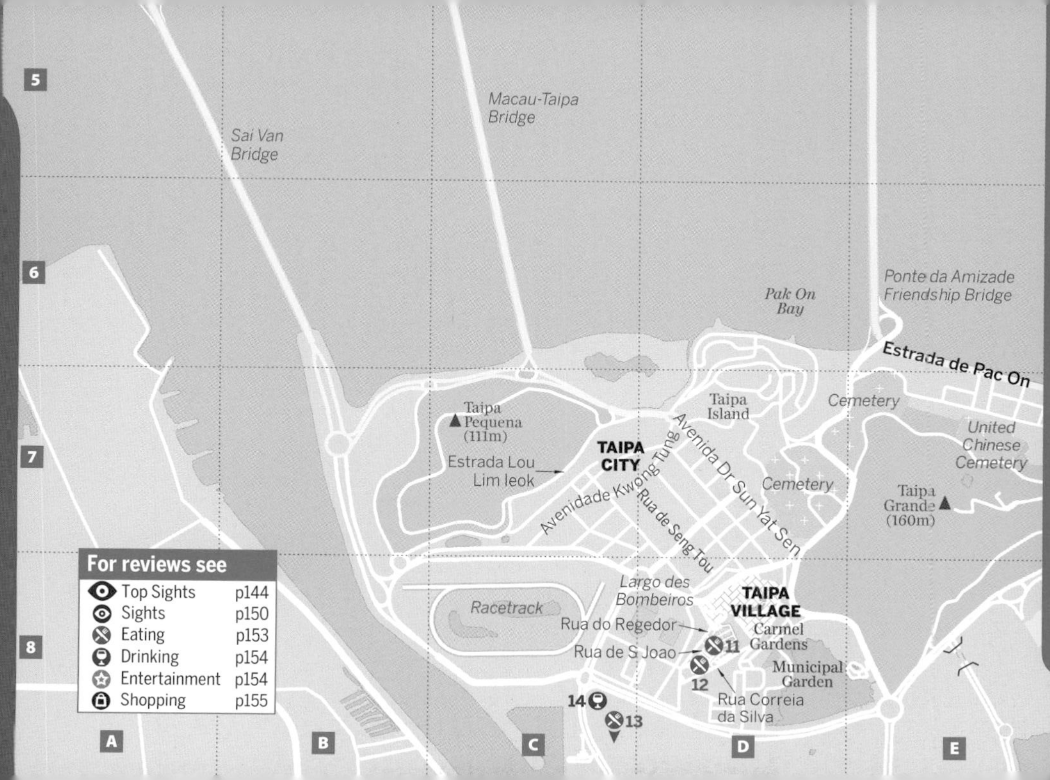

Ponte da Amizade
Friendship Bridge

Estrada de Pac On

United
Chinese
Cemetery

Taipa
Grande ▲
(160m)

Cemetery

Puk On
Bay

Cemetery

Taipa
Island

Avenida Dr Sun Yat Sen

Rua de Seng Tou

TAIPA
VILLAGE

Carmel
Gardens

🚇11

Municipal
Garden

Rua Correia
da Silva

12 🍴

Macau-Taipa
Bridge

TAIPA
CITY

Avenida Kwong Tung

Largo des
Bombeiros

Rua do Regedor

Rua de S Joao

14 🍴   🍴13

Taipa
Pequena ▲
(111m)

Estrada Lou
Lim Ieok

Racetrack

Sai Van
Bridge

For reviews see	
⊙ Top Sights	p144
◉ Sights	p150
✖ Eating	p153
🍷 Drinking	p154
Entertainment	p154
🛍 Shopping	p155

5

6

7

8

A   B   C   D   E

Sights

A-Ma Temple

TEMPLE

1 Map p148, A4

Macau's oldest temple (1488) is named after the goddess of the sea, better known as Tin Hau. It was probably standing when the Portuguese arrived, although the present building may only date back to the 17th century. At the entrance is a large boulder with a coloured relief of a *lorcha,* a traditional sailing vessel of the South China Sea. (媽閣廟; Templo de A-Ma; Rua de São Tiago da Barra; admission free; ⊙10am-6pm; 🚍1, 2, 5, 10, 21A)

Macau Museum of Art

MUSEUM

2 Map p148, D3

This vast, excellent museum houses rotating exhibits as well as permanent collections of works by established Chinese and Western artists. The Shiwan pottery collection is one of the world's best. (澳門藝術博物館; Museu de Arte de Macau; www.mam.gov.mo; Macau Cultural Centre, Avenida Xian Xing Hai; admission MOP$5; ⊙10am-6.30pm Tue-Sun; 🚍1A, 8)

AFA (Art for All Society)

GALLERY

3 Map p148, C1

Macau's very best contemporary art can be seen at this nonprofit gallery, founded in 2007 by a local artist. The gallery is located near the Mong Ha Multi-Sport Pavilion (望廈體育館); it's a little over 1km from Largo do Senado. (全藝社; ☎2836 6064; www.afamacau.com; 10th fl, Edifio da Fabrica de Baterias NE National, 52 Estrada da Areia Preta; admission free; ⊙noon-7pm Mon-Sat; 🚍7, 8)

Guia Fort

FORTRESS

4 Map p148, C2

Situated on the highest point of the peninsula, Macau's most significant fort is home to the oldest lighthouse on the China coast (built in 1865) and

Local Life

Macau's Sword Master

The charismatic **Antonio Conceição Junior** (www.arscives.com/bladesign; antonio.cejunior@gmail.com) is Macau's best-known designer. He has a vast repertoire spanning Macau postage stamps, fashion, jewellery, medallions and book covers.

Antonio also designs custom swords inspired by Macanese and ancient cultures, mythology and the modern world – both Eastern (*katana* and *tantō*) and Western (sabres and cutlasses) blades, as well as hybrids.

Antonio can recommend bladesmiths in North America to manufacture and ship the swords. Email him for enquiries; expect about one to two weeks for the completed design and a fee of about US$3000.

the stunning **Chapel of Our Lady of Guia** (聖母雪地殿教堂; Capela de Nossa Señora da Guia; ⏱10am-5pm Tue-Sun), built in 1622 and retaining almost all of its original features, including some of Asia's most valuable mural paintings. (東望洋山堡壘; Fortaleza de Guia; admission free; ⏱9am-5.30pm; 🚍2, 17)

Kun Iam Temple

TEMPLE

5 🔘 Map p148, C1

In the main hall of Macau's second-oldest temple (1627) is a statue of a bearded arhat rumoured to represent Marco Polo. The first treaty of trade and friendship between the USA and China was signed in the temple's gardens in 1844. (觀音堂; Templo de Kun Iam; Avenida do Coronel Mesquita; ⏱10am-6pm; 🚍12, 17, 18)

Monte Fort & Macau Museum

FORTRESS, MUSEUM

6 🔘 Map p148, B2

Housed in the remarkable 17th-century **Monte Fort** (admission free; ⏱7am-7pm), this worthwhile museum tells an engaging tale of the history of Macau and is perhaps the best introduction to its traditions and culture. (澳門博物館; Museu de Macau; www.macaumuseum.gov.mo; Praceta do Museu de Macau, Fortaleza do Monte; MOP$15; ⏱10am-5.30pm Tue-Sun; 🚍7, 8)

BRUCE YUANYUE BI/GETTY IMAGES ©

A-Ma Temple

Mandarin's House

NOTABLE BUILDING

7 🔘 Map p148, A3

This stunning complex (c 1869), with more than 60 rooms, was the ancestral home of Zheng Guanying, an author-merchant whose readers included Chairman Mao. There's a moon gate, a passageway for sedans, and courtyards and halls in a labyrinthine layout. (鄭家大屋; Caso do Mandarim; 📞2896 8820; www.wh.mo/mandarinhouse; 10 Travessa de Antonio da Silva; admission free; ⏱10am-5.30pm Fri-Tue; 🚍28B, 16)

Understand

Mediterrasian Macau

The Portuguese colonisation of Macau, which lasted from the mid-16th century to 1999, left a legacy of southern European–style buildings in the Chinese city. But what appears to be Portuguese architecture is often a complex fusion of Portuguese and Chinese building styles, techniques and materials, with influences from Goa (India), the Philippines and Malacca (Malaysia) – as well as contributions from the Italian and Spanish missionaries who enriched it with their sensibilities and traditions. Generally the only buildings that are entirely Chinese or Portuguese are, respectively, temples and fortresses.

Churches

Macau's churches feature a baroque style simplified and adapted for the tropical climate, similar to that found in Goa and Brazil. A characteristic of this tropicalised baroque architecture is the use of wood in place of stone – the Chinese were experts at carpentry, while the southern Europeans were master masons.

You can see this at St Joseph Seminary Church (p145), one of Macau's most beautiful buildings. Consecrated in 1758, it has a lemon-meringue facade, a scalloped canopy at the entrance and the first dome to be built in all of China. Inside, you'll find decorations made of plaster – common in this part of the world – and a timber roof propped up by a Chinese system of triangular beams and rafters, and covered with Guangdong tiles attached by cement for protection against tropical monsoons.

The Church of St Dominic (p145) has light-wooden balconies and wide-open windows, both characteristics of a hot climate.

See p144 for a discussion of Asian influences in the Church of St Paul.

Residences

The Mandarin's House (p151), a Qing-dynasty Southern Chinese residential complex, has Western-style arches and window panels inlaid with mother-of-pearl, a technique of ornamentation also practised in India, the Philippines and Turkey.

St Lazarus Church District
NEIGHBOURHOOD

8 Map p148, B2

This lovely neighbourhood has cobbled streets where artists like to set up shop. Highlights include **Old Ladies' House** (仁慈堂婆仔屋; www.albcreativelab.com; 8 Calcada da Igreja de Sao Lazaro; admission free; ⊗noon-7pm Wed-Mon), which once sheltered homeless elderly women; and **Tai Fung Tong Art House** (大瘋堂藝舍; 7 Calcada Central de Sao Lazaro; admission free; ⊗2-6pm Tue-Sun), a historical building featuring a mix of Chinese and European architectural styles. (瘋堂斜巷; Calcada da Igreja de Sao Lazaro; 🚌7, 8)

Eating

Alfonso III
MACANESE $

9 Map p148, B3

With a diverse menu featuring liver and tripe dishes in addition to popular classics – all fabulously executed – it's clear that this low-key eatery doesn't just cater for the weekend crowds. Book ahead; it's always packed. (亞豐素三世餐廳; 🕿2858 6272; 11a Rua Central, Macau; meals from MOP$200; ⊗lunch & dinner Mon-Sat; 🚌6, 9, 16)

☑️ Top Tip
Casino Shuttles

All big-name casinos have free shuttle services to and from the ferry terminals, the border gate into mainland China and the airport. Anyone can use these buses no questions asked (some rides even come with free chips!). You'll see them outside the ferry terminals and the casinos. For border gate and airport routes, enquire at the casinos.

Restaurante Litoral
MACANESE $$

10 Map p148, A3

This is arguably the best Macanese restaurant on the peninsula; it offers superb duck and baked rice dishes. (海灣餐廳; 🕿2896 7878; 261A Rua do Almirante Sérgio, Macau; meals from MOP$200; ⊗lunch & dinner; 🚌14, 61)

A Petisqueira
PORTUGUESE $

11 Map p148, D8

This unassuming eatery favoured by the Macanese community has been whipping up authentic Portuguese dishes for almost two decades. Book ahead. (葡國美食天地; 🕿2882 5354; 15D, 15C Rua de S Joao, Taipa Village; meals from MOP$180; ⊗lunch & dinner Tue-Sun; 🚌11, 15, 22)

Antonio PORTUGUESE $$$

12 Map p148, D8

Dark mahogany and blue-and-white *azulejo* tiles prepare you for an authentic Portuguese meal at this Michelin-recommended restaurant known for its seafood stew and goat's-milk cheese with olive oil and honey. (安东尼奥; ☑2899 9998; www.antonio macau.com; 3 Rua dos Negociantes, Taipa Village; meals MOP$250-1200; ☺lunch & dinner Mon-Fri, noon-10.30pm Sat & Sun; ☐11, 15, 22)

Café Nga Tim MACANESE $$

13 Map p148, C8

We love Nga Tim's simple and traditional Chinese-Portuguese food, its laid-back atmosphere, location (opposite the Chapel of St Francis Xavier in Coloane, see p147), prices and especially the owner – Feeling, a guitar-and *èrhú* (mandolin)-strumming former cop. (雅憩花園餐廳; ☑2888 2086; 8 Rua Caetano, Coloane Village; meals MOP$70-200; ☺noon-1am; ☐15, 21A, 25)

Drinking

Corner's Wine Bar & Tapas Café WINE BAR

This rooftop wine bar has a great location just across from the Ruins of the Church of St Paul (see ◉ Map p148, B2) and serves decent tapas dishes. It's most atmospheric at night. (☑2848

2848; 3 Travessa de São Paulo, Macau; ☺cafe noon-5pm daily, bar 5pm-midnight Sun-Thu, to 1am Fri & Sat; ☐8A, 17, 26)

Macallan Whisky Bar & Lounge WHISKY BAR

14 Map p148, C8

Arguably the best whisky bar in Macau, this handsome place features lots of oak panels, Jacobean rugs and a working fireplace. The 400-plus whisky labels hail from Ireland, France, Sweden and India – not to mention a Scottish 1963 Glemorangie. (Rm 203, 2nd fl, Galaxy Hotel, Avenida de Cotai, Taipa Village; ☺5pm-1am Mon-Thu, to 2am Fri & Sat; ☐25,25X)

Entertainment

Grand Lisboa CASINO

15 Map p148, B3

Packed with rare artworks and precious stones, the lavish and spectacular Grand Lisboa's towering, flaming torch–shaped megastructure is home to the best-known casino in Macau, which was opened by a local mogul (as opposed to brandname imports such as Wynn). It's also a handy landmark for nagivating the peninsula's streets. (www.grandlisboa.com; Avenida de Lisboa, Macau; ☺24hr)

Macau Soul LIVE MUSIC

Huddled in the shadows of the Ruins of the Church of St Paul (see ◉ Map p148,

Grand Lisboa

B2), Macau Soul is elegantly decked out in woods and stained-glass windows, with a basement where blues bands perform to packed audiences. Opening hours vary, so phone ahead. (澳感廊; ☏2836 5182; www.macausoul.com; 31A Rua de Sao Paulo, Macau; ⊙to 9.15pm Mon, Tue, Thu, to 11.15pm Fri-Sun, closed Wed; 🚌8A, 17)

Shopping

Macau Creations   GIFTS

This shop, under the Ruins of St Paul (see ◉ Map p148, B2), features excellent Macau-themed clothes, stationery and other memorabilia designed by 30 artists living in the city, including the brilliant Russian painter Konstantin Bessmertny. (澳門佳作; ☏2835 2954; www.macaucreations.com; 5a Rua da Ressurreicao, Macau; ⊙10am-10pm; 🚌8A, 17, 26)

Mercearia
Portuguesa   FOOD, JEWELLERY

This charming shop near Restaurante Litoral (see 10 ✗ Map p148, A3), owned by a film director and an actress (both Portuguese), has a small but well-curated selection of provisions, such as jams, soaps, chinaware, gold jewellery, wooden toys and bath products from Portugal. (☏2856 2708; www.mercearia portuguesa.com; 8 Calcada da Igreja de Sao Lazaro, Macau; ⊙noon-8pm; 🚌7, 8)

The Best of
Hong Kong

Hong Kong's Best Walks

Hong Kong's Best...

Dada (p108)
KYLIE MCLAUGHLIN/GETTY IMAGES ©

Best Walks
Postwar Buildings & Colonial Life in Tsim Sha Tsui

The Walk

In the early days of the colony, Tsim Sha Tsui (TST) was a garden city inhabited by Europeans. Nathan Rd was lined on both sides by colonial houses. Chinese banyans, some of which you can still see today, were planted to provide shade. Chinese were not allowed to live in TST until the early 20th century when the area was being developed into a hub of trade and tourism. After the Communist takeover in 1949, many Shanghainese businessmen fled to Hong Kong; some settled in TST. In the northern part of the district today, you'll see postwar buildings that were once homes to this Chinese ethnic group.

Start Former Kowloon British School; Ⓜ Jordan, exit A

Finish Jordan Path; Ⓜ Jordan, exit A

Length 2.5km; two hours

✕ Take a Break

Drop by **Chicken HOF & Soju Korean** (李家 Chicken; ☏ 2375 8080; 84 Kam Kok Mansion, Kimberley Rd, Tsim Sha Tsui; meals from $150) as you make your way to Chatham Rd South from Austin Ave.

St Andrew's Church

❶ Former Kowloon British School

To reach this former school (p100), turn right from exit B1 of Tsim Sha Tsui MTR station and walk north along Nathan Rd. Next door is **St Andrew's Church** (p99), Kowloon's oldest Anglican church. Further north on Nathan Rd, turn right into Austin Rd, a former stronghold of Shanghainese migrants.

❷ Pak On Building

Explore **Pak On Building** (百安大廈) with its lobby arcade littered with shops, including, down near Tak Shing St, a liquor store that stocks absinthe. Further down, where Austin Rd branches into Austin Ave, there's a late-1960s building with rounded balconies spiralling skyward.

❸ Carnival Mansion

Carnival Mansion (嘉華 大廈) has a courtyard where you can stare up at a vortex of rickety postwar homes. Inside are yellow terrazzo stairs with green balustrades made by Shanghainese craftsmen half a century ago.

④ Success Stationery

Next door is **Success** (成功文具行) stationery shop, run by Ray and Philip since the '70s. You'll also spot the curious **'triangular public toilet'** (三角公廁). Continue down Austin Ave and make a left on Chatham Rd South. **Rosary Church** (玫瑰堂) is Kowloon's oldest Catholic church.

⑤ Gun Club Hill Barracks

At the big junction, make a left into Austin Rd. The canon-guarded gates of **Gun Club Hill Barracks** (槍會山軍營), now home to the People's Liberation Army (PLA), is on its other side. Turn into the leafy alley (**Jordan Path**) just next to the gates.

⑥ Jordan Path

Note how functional buildings loom up on your right, while mani-

cured lawns of colonial recreation clubs unfurl on your left. As you near Jordan Rd, you'll see **PLA hospital** (解放軍駐軍醫院) with its darkened windows. Crossing Cox's Rd takes you to Victorian-style, Anglican **Kowloon Union Church** (c 1927) (九龍佑寧堂). Continue along Jordan Rd for Jordan MTR station.

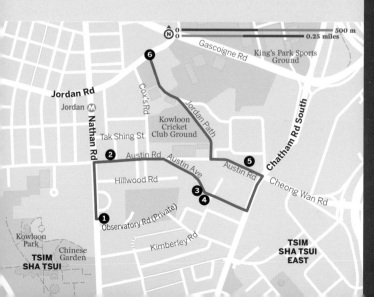

Best Walks
Wan Chai's Forgotten Streets

The Walk

Wan Chai's old coastline used to run near the tram tracks on Johnston Rd before zealous land reclamation pushed the shoreline to the north. During that time, the area around Queen's Rd East and Johnston Rd was a small fishing village with shrines and temples overlooking the sea. After the British came, shipyards were built along the bay and 'second-rank' Europeans who could not afford to live on Victoria Peak made their homes on the hills south of Queen's Rd East. Now that area still contains some of Wan Chai's most exclusive real estate. Though new Wan Chai is an exciting commercial district with gleaming skyscrapers and five-star hotels, for those keen on exploration, the south side of the (tram) tracks will always be more interesting.

Start Pak Tai Temple; **M** Wan Chai, exit A3

Finish Star St; **M** Admiralty, exit F

Length 1.2km; two hours

✗ Take a Break

La Creperie (p75)

Classified Mozzarella Bar

① Pak Tai Temple

A five-minute stroll south from Wan Chai MTR station, past Johnston Rd, lies stunning **Pak Tai Temple** (p70), built 150 years ago by local residents.

② Hong Kong House of Stories

Further down the slope on Stone Nullah Lane, the **Hong Kong House of Stories** (p71), aka the Blue House, will show you what life was like in Wan Chai in the last century (the house has no toilet-flushing facilities). It was painted blue during a renovation in the 1920s because the government had surplus blue paint.

③ Old Wan Chai Post Office

Head west on Queen's Rd East and glance across at the **streamline moderne facade** of a shopping centre that used to be the Wan Chai Market. Once the neighbourhood hub, the market was used as a mortuary by Japanese forces in WWII. The pocket-sized **Old Wan Chai Post Office** (p71) is Hong Kong's oldest.

❹ Spring Garden Lane

Cross the road to take a look at **Spring Garden Lane**, one of the first areas developed by the British. A British merchant had a lavish residence here named Spring Gardens, and Spring Garden Lane was the length between its north and south gates. In the 1900s, the lane harboured many brothels.

❺ Ghost House

Come back to the southern side of Queen's Rd East. Peep inside mysterious **Hung Shing Temple** (p70), once a seaside shrine. Just west of the temple turn up the hill along Ship St and stand before the now-derelict **Ghost House** at 55 Nam Koo Terrace. Its history is a wretched one: it was used by Japanese soldiers as a brothel housing 'comfort women' in WWII.

❻ Star Street

Star St neighbourhood is a quiet corner that contains the old – including a family-run *dai pai dong* (hawker-style food stall) on St Francis St – and the new – quaint boutiques, cafes and restaurants. Just above **Classified Mozzarella Bar** (p76) is a six-storey balconied building in art-deco style. At the junction of Wing Fung St and Queen's Rd East you'll see a building with signage to the Admiralty MTR station just under it.

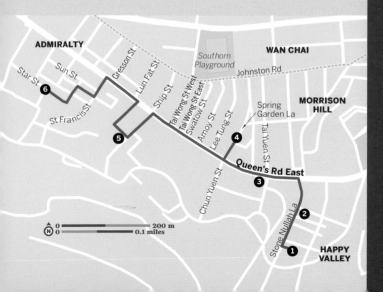

Best Walks
Wholesale District (Sheung Wan)

The Walk

Sheung Wan became a trading hub in the mid-19th century, when turmoil in China caused many Chinese businessmen, notably from Chaozhou (Chiu Chow) in Guangdong province, to flee to the territory. With their capital, they set up businesses in Sheung Wan, trading in dried seafood, Chinese herbs and rice. Not everyone who arrived was rich though. The majority worked as coolies at the piers. As more and more migrants came, the area around Tai Ping Shan St became the heart of the Chinese community, with its own places of worship and funeral parlours. Sheung Wan was also tied to Sun Yat-sen, aka 'Father of Modern China', who went to school as a teenager here and, later, held secret meetings as a revolutionary.

Start Kennedy Town tram (Sutherland St stop)

Finish 🚌26, Hollywood Rd; Ⓜ Sheung Wan, entrance/exit B

Length 1.9km; one hour

✕ Take a Break
Doppio Zero Trattoria (p37)

HOLGER LEUE/GETTY IMAGES ©
Dried seafood shop

❶ Dried Seafood Shops

From the Sutherland St stop of the Kennedy Town tram, have a look at (and a sniff of) Des Voeux Rd West's many **dried seafood shops** piled with all manner of desiccated sea life - scallops, abalone, sea cucumber, oysters, conch and fish maw.

❷ Herbal-Medicine Traders

Head south on Ko Shing St, to browse the positively medieval-sounding goods on offer from the **herbal-medicine traders**. At the end of Ko Shing St, re-enter Des Voeux Rd West and walk northeast. Continue along Connaught Rd Central, where you'll pass the Edwardian building housing the **Western Market**.

❸ Ginseng and Bird's Nest Shops

At the corner of Morrison St, walk south to Wing Lok St and Bonham Strand, which are both lined with shops selling **ginseng and edible bird's nests**, the latter made from the salivary excretions of cave swifts, and consumed (as a sweet soup) for their proven ability to regenerate human cells.

❹ Tai Ping Shan Temples

Turn right onto Queen's Rd Central and pass by shops selling **paper funeral offerings for the dead**. Climb up Possession St, then take a right into Hollywood Rd, a left into Po Yan St and then a left into **Tai Ping Shan Street** (p35), where you'll spot three temples. Look to the right for **Pak Sing Ancestral Hall** and **Kwun Yum Temple**, and to the left for **Tai Sui Temple**.

❺ Antique Shops

Head up Upper Station St to the start of Hollywood Rd's **antique shops**. There's a vast choice of curios, replicas and a few rare, mostly Chinese, treasures.

❻ Man Mo Temple

Continuing east on Hollywood Rd brings you to **Man Mo Temple** (p28) one of the oldest temples in the territory and dedicated to the civil and martial gods Man Cheung and Kwan Yu. From here catch bus 26 or head north towards the harbour for Sheung Wan MTR station on Des Voeux Rd.

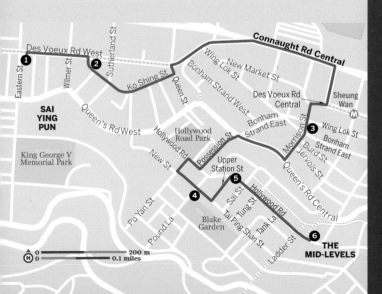

Best
Views

Best Eye-Level Views

Star Ferry (p26) There's no better way to view Hong Kong's famous harbour.

Trams (p76) Turn the city into a carousel of moving images.

Happy Valley Racecourse (p64) Between mountains and high-rises, the ponies gallop.

Best Vantage Points

Tsim Sha Tsui East Promenade (p96) Face to face with Hong Kong's most iconic view.

Hong Kong Monetary Authority Information Centre (p32) Sweeping 55th-floor vistas by the edge of the water, inside Two IFC.

Bank of China Tower (p32) Views stretch all the way to Kowloon from the 42nd floor.

Best Views from a Bar

Sevva (p39) So close to the HSBC Building, it's downright dizzying.

Felix (p108) Awesome views of Tsim Sha Tsui, especially from the men's bathroom.

InterContinental Lobby Lounge (p108) Same as Tsim Sha Tsui East Promenade but with air-con.

Aqua Spirit (p107) A dramatic take on the Island skyline, especially at night.

Best Mountain-Top Views

Tian Tan Buddha (p138) See luxuriant Lantau island from 523m above the sea.

Tai Long Wan Trail (p131) Billowing hills and secluded coves.

Tung Ping Chau (p131) Cliffs with strange rocks hang over surf-beaten beaches.

NAKI KOUYIOUMTZIS/GETTY IMAGES ©

Best Views from a Park

Victoria Peak (pictured above; p58) Revisit the city from top down.

Hong Kong Park (p62) Unique juxtaposition of skyscrapers and mountains.

Ocean Park (p89) Its cable cars command views of the peaceful South China Sea.

Best
Temples

LONELY PLANET/GETTY IMAGES ©

Most Historically Important

Tsing Shan Monastery
(p135) Believed to be the founding site of Buddhism in Hong Kong.

Po Lin Monastery
(p139) Formerly also known as 'Buddhist Kingdom in the South'.

Kun Iam Temple, Macau
(p151) An important treaty was signed here in 1844.

Man Mo Temple (p28) Once a court of arbitration for the Chinese.

Oldest Temples

A-Ma Temple, Macau
(p150) Macau's oldest temple was originally established in 1488.

Kun Iam Temple, Macau (p151) Macau's second-oldest temple (c 1627).

Tsing Shan Monastery
(p135) Said to have been built in the Jin dynasty (1115–1234).

Best Non-Taoist Temples

Tsing Shan Monastery
(p135) One of Hong Kong's three oldest temples is modest and charming.

Khalsa Diwan Sikh Temple (p67) Hong Kong's largest Sikh temple.

Chi Lin Nunnery (p127) Wonderful faux-Tang dynasty architecture c 1998.

Best Urban Temples

Tin Hau Temple (p117) Right in Yau Ma Tei's community hub.

Man Mo Temple (p28) This famous temple sits in Sheung Wan.

Pak Tai Temple (p70) Magnificent (and in Wan Chai).

Fook Tak Ancient Temple (p99) Tsim Sha Tsui's only temple.

Quirkiest Temples

Hung Shing Temple
(pictured above; p70) Dark, mysterious, sits on a boulder.

Pak Sing Ancestral Hall (p35) Where bodies awaiting repatriation to China were kept.

Fook Tak Ancient Temple (p99) A tiny and smoky former shrine.

Temples with the Most Visual Impact

Sik Sik Yuen Wong Tai Sin Temple (p126) Colourful and flamboyant.

Man Mo Temple (p28) Incense coils hang from the ceiling.

Tian Tan Buddha (p138) The world's tallest seated outdoor bronze Buddha.

Best
Architecture

Over the centuries Hong Kong has played host to everything from Tao temples and Qing dynasty forts to Victorian churches and Edwardian hotels. But Hong Kong's ceaseless cycle of deconstruction and reconstruction, up until recently at least, has meant that the old and charming are often eagerly replaced by modern marvels, at least in the central parts of the city.

PHOTO: ALLAN BAXTER/GETTY IMAGES ©

BANK OF CHINA ARCHITECT: IM PEI

Traditional Chinese

About the only examples of precolonial Chinese architecture left in urban Hong Kong are Tin Hau temples that date from the early to mid-19th century, including those at Tin Hau near Causeway Bay and Yau Ma Tei. For anything more substantial, you have to go to the New Territories, where walled villages, fortresses and ancient pagodas can be seen.

Colonial Architecture

Most of what is left of colonial architecture is on Hong Kong Island, especially in Central, where the seat of the government is located, though Tsim Sha Tsui on the Kowloon Peninsula also boasts quite a few examples. Some of Hong Kong's colonial architecture features adaptations for the tropical climate, just as some Chinese buildings have Western motifs. But Hong Kong's examples of hybrid architecture pale in comparison to what is available in Macau.

Modern Architecture

Enthusiasts of modern architecture will have a field day here. Central and Wan Chai on Hong Kong Island are especially rich showcases for the modern and contemporary buildings – many designed by internationally celebrated architects such as Norman Foster and IM Pei.

☑ **Top Tips**

► For a list of historic structures, visit the website of the **Hong Kong Antiquities & Monuments Office** (☎ 2721 2326; www .amo.gov.hk; 136 Nathan Rd, Tsim Sha Tsui; ⏰ 9am-5pm Mon-Sat) or in person – it's inside the **Former Kowloon British School** (p100) in Tsim Sha Tsui.

► For the latest in Hong Kong's preservation efforts, see www.heritage .gov.hk.

St Joseph's Seminary Church (p145), Macau

Best Pre-Colonial Chinese Buildings

Man Mo Temple (p28) Built in the 1800s by wealthy Chinese merchants.

Ping Shan Heritage Trail (p135) The magnificent ancestral hall here dates to the 1300s.

Tin Hau Temple (p117) Built by fishermen and relocated here in 1876.

Best Colonial Structures

Central Police Station Compound (p47) Featuring a late-Victorian style, among others.

Former Marine Police Headquarters (p100) One of the oldest (c 1884) and handsomest government buildings still around.

Former Kowloon British School (p100) The oldest surviving school building (c 1902) for expat children.

Clock Tower (p97) The only remaining structure (c 1915) of the old Kowloon–Canton Railway.

Best Contemporary Buildings

HSBC Building (p24) Masterpiece in late-modern, high-tech style by Norman Foster.

Bank of China Tower (pictured above left; p32) A wonderful tower of cubes by IM Pei.

Asia Society Hong Kong Centre (p70) Sublime complex designed by Billie Tsien and Tod Williams.

Best Fusion Architecture

Ruins of the Church of St Paul, Macau (p144) Southern European with Asian details; 16th century.

St Joseph's Seminary Church, Macau (p145) Arguably Macau's best example of tropicalised baroque (mid-18th-century) architecture.

Mandarin's House, Macau (p151) Graceful Chinese residence with hints of European influence.

Former Kowloon British School (p100) Victorian in style but adapted for a hot and humid climate.

Best
Museums &
Galleries

Best Collections

Hong Kong Heritage Museum (p134) Permanent exhibitions on the New Territories and Cantonese opera.

Hong Kong Museum of Art (p97) Chinese art from Han to Qing dynasties, as well as Hong Kong art.

Hong Kong Museum of History (pictured right; p99) Overview of the history and customs of Hong Kong.

Macau Museum of Art (p150) Works by Macau's Chinese, Macanese and Western artists, and Shiwan pottery.

Best Buyable Art

Grotto Fine Art (p56) One of very few galleries with a focus on the best Hong Kong art.

10 Chancery Lane Gallery (p57) Thought-provoking works from China, Asia, Europe and Hong Kong.

AFA (Art for All Society), Macau (p150) Excellent works by Macau's top artists.

Sin Sin Fine Art (p40) Edgy contemporary art from Europe and Asia.

Best 'People's' Art Spaces

Para/Site Art Space (p35) Arguably Hong Kong's best nonprofit art space.

Jockey Club Creative Arts Centre (p127) Artists' studios in a breezy former factory.

C&G Artpartment (p119) A socially-minded art space in the middle of Mong Kok.

Most Entertaining

Flagstaff Museum of Tea Ware (p63) Featuring prized Chinese tea ware donated by a private collector.

Hong Kong Science Museum (p97) From gravity to tadpoles, all worldly phenomena explained.

Hong Kong Space Museum (p97) Try 'moonwalking' and eating astronaut ice-cream.

☑ Top Tips

▶ **Hong Kong Art Walk** (www.hongkongartwalk.com) features some 60 galleries on the Island opening their doors and entertaining with food and wine for one night in March.

▶ **Art Basel Hong Kong** (http://hongkong.artbasel.com) in May sees hundreds of galleries and dealers from the world over participating to attract new buyers and collectors.

▶ **Fotanian** (www.fotanian.com) is an open-studio event in January in former factory premises in Fo Tan, New Territories.

Best
Parks &
Gardens

Best for Wildlife

Hong Kong Wetland Park (p134) Watch migratory birds in a natural setting.

Mai Po Marsh Nature Reserve (p135) For 380 species of birds.

Hong Kong Park (pictured right; p62) Large aviary where you can view birds from different angles.

Hong Kong Zoological & Botanical Gardens (p33) A collection of birds, beasts and plants.

Best for Manmade Beauty

Victoria Peak Garden (p59) Restored 'Victorian' garden of a former governor's summer lodge.

Tsim Sha Tsui East Waterfront Podium Garden (p101) Granite edifices and white sail shades.

Hong Kong Park (p62) Artificial waterfalls and ponds furnished with real waterfowl.

Best for People-Watching

Middle Road Children's Playground (p101) Breezy park frequented by all ages and ethnicities.

Kowloon Park (p102) Locals come to chat, picnic, swim, jog and practise kung fu.

Victoria Park (p73) Hang-out of Chinese families and, on Sundays, Indonesian domestic helpers.

Ocean Park (p89) During holidays it's packed with locals and tourists.

Most Secluded

Lan Kwai Fong Amphitheatre (p44) Where Lan Kwai Fong's revellers go for some quiet.

Victoria Peak Garden (p58) Serene and romantic.

Mai Po Marsh Nature Reserve (p135) Birds are louder than people here, most of the time.

Middle Road Children's Playground (p101) There are very few people here on weekdays.

☑ Top Tip

▶ For a longer list of Hong Kong's green green grass, visit http://lawnmap.org

Best for a Picnic

Victoria Peak Garden (p58) Tea-party in style at this faux-Victorian garden with gazebos.

Victoria Park (p73) No shortage of plush blades where you can soak up the sun.

Kowloon Park (p102) Take your pick from lawn, bench or concrete at this former barracks.

Best
Shops

Everyone knows Hong Kong as a place of neon-lit retail pilgrimage. This city is positively stuffed with swanky shopping malls and brand-name boutiques. These are supplemented by the city's own retail trailblazers and creative local designers.

Clothing

The best place to find designer brands and luxury stores is in the malls. For something more unique, there are cool independent stores opened by local designers and retailers, especially in Sheung Wan, Wan Chai and Tsim Sha Tsui. You'll see some brilliant pieces but the range is limited simply because these places are few and far between. The best hunting grounds for low-cost garments are the street markets.

Electronics

One of the cheapest places in the world for electronics and digitals, Hong Kong has a plethora of gadget shops. As a rule of thumb do not buy from street-level shops on Nathan Rd. The camera shops and computer malls listed in this book are generally honest, though some shops in computer malls have been known to sell used items as new.

Antiques

Hong Kong has a rich array of Asian antiques on offer, especially Chinese, but expert reproductions abound. Serious buyers will restrict themselves to reputable antique shops and auction houses such as Christie's, especially at its auctions in spring and autumn when you'll find some excellent authentic pieces.

☑ **Top Tips**

▶ There's no sales tax in Hong Kong for most goods.

▶ Direct complaints to Hong Kong Tourism Board's **Quality Tourism Services** (☎2806 2823; www.qtshk.com) or **Hong Kong Consumer Council** (☎2929 2222; www.consumer.org.hk; ⊗Mon-Fri 9am-5.45pm).

Best for Fashion

Daydream Nation (p81) Edgy and romantic streetwear by Kay Wong.

Initial (p110) European- and Japanese-influenced local fashion.

Horizon Plaza (p93) Twenty-eight floors of fashion and furniture.

High-end women's fashion at Pacific Place mall (p81)

Johnna Ho (p110) Smart and chic women's wear.

Best for Period Pieces

Arch Angel Antiques (p56) Tombware, urns and smaller pieces.

Honeychurch Antiques (p57) Chinese furniture and European pieces.

Wattis Fine Art (p57) Ancient maps and old photos.

Best for Souvenirs

G.O.D. (p81) Hip, retro, design-oriented goods.

Shanghai Tang (p40) Clothes and homeware in modern chinoiserie style.

Yue Hwa Chinese Products Emporium (p124) Chinese-style silk gowns, furniture, knick-knacks.

Most Specialised

Bruce Lee Club (p123) Shop and mini-museum devoted to the kung-fu icon.

Guitar Sofa (p125) New and used guitars and amps.

Fook Ming Tong Tea Shop (p40) Good Chinese tea.

Best for Digital Gadgets

Wan Chai Computer Centre (p82) Almost everything computer-related.

Photo Scientific (p57) Professional photographers shop here.

Ap Liu Street Flea Market (p127) New and used electronics, including batteries and toys.

David Chan Photo Shop (p110) Mint-condition vintage cameras.

Best Speciality Malls

Rise Shopping Arcade (p111) Heaving with tiny fashion and accessory boutiques.

Sino Centre (p123) Manga, speciality magazines, used CDs.

Sin Tat Plaza (p124) Mobile phones, including secondhand and knock-offs.

Best **Activities**

Most Scenic Hiking Trails

High Island Reservoir East Dam Trail (p130) Natural and manmade sublimity.

Tai Long Wan Trail (p131) A popular route with views of secluded beaches.

Shing Mun Reservoir Trail (p131) A serene reservoir surrounded by paper-bark trees.

Best Heritage Trails

Bride's Pool – Lai Chi Wo (p131) Large Hakka village and well-preserved 'feng shui' forest.

Ma On Shan Country Park Trail (p131) Passes an old iron miners' settlement.

Tung Ping Chau Walking Trail (p131) Volcanic rock formations from aeons ago.

Shing Mun Reservoir Trail (p131) Reservoir structures are a listed heritage.

Best Beaches

South Bay (p87) A gem of a beach, especially at night.

Middle Bay (p87) A quaint beach popular with scenesters.

St Stephen's Beach (p87) Close to Stanley but without the crowds.

Best for Meeting People

Salsa, tango or swing (p55) Party with locals and expats at club nights.

Taichi (p108) Other travellers will likely be taking the same class.

Southorn Playground (p66) At any time of the day you'll meet locals from different walks of life.

Best for Pampering

Happy Foot Reflexology (p48) Foot and body massage.

Ten Feet Tall (p39) Feet kneading in a design-oriented parlour.

MARK HANNAFORD/GETTY IMAGES ©

☑ **Top Tips**

▶ **Hong Kong Ultimate Frisbee Association** (www.hkupa.com) has twice-a-week pick-ups, and a major Hat Tournament (accompanied by much partying) in May.

▶ **Casual Football Network** (http://casualfootball.net) has at least three games of football (soccer) a week.

▶ **Natural Excursion Ideals** (☎9300 5197; www.kayak-and-hike.com) runs hiking and kayaking trips.

Sense of Touch (p48) Luxurious massages and superfluous treatments.

Best **Markets**

Best Speciality Markets

Cat Street Bazaar (p35) Curios and (mostly) faux period pieces outdoors and in shops.

Jade Market (p117) Jade pendants, bracelets and other accessories in a covered setting.

Ap Liu Street Flea Market (p127) Electronic and digital gadgets, used and new; in stalls and outdoors.

Best for Fresh Food

Graham Street Market (pictured above right; p47) Fruit, veggie, meat and seafood market along the street.

Wan Chai's Markets (p82) Fresh food, noodles and spices along the street.

Ap Lei Chau Market Cooked Food Centre (p90) Huge selection of live fish and crustaceans inside a building.

Best for Clothing

Stanley Market (p87) Tees, children's wear, Chinese-style garb in a maze of shops.

Tung Choi Street (Ladies') Market (p124) Cheap casual clothing in stalls lining a street.

Li Yuen Street East & West (p41) Hawkers selling clothes, shoes and handbags crammed into alleyways.

Best for Atmosphere

Temple Street Night Market (p114) A sensory journey under the moon.

Yau Ma Tei Wholesale Fruit Market (p118) These historic buildings come alive in the wee hours.

Graham Street Market (p47) Cheerful and local, with a great range of produce.

Wan Chai's Markets (p82) The shops and stalls here are positively buzzing with local life.

TIM GRAHAM/ALAMY ©

Most Eclectic Markets

Temple Street Night Market (p114) Fortune tellers, Cantonese opera performers, hawkers, hookers and street food.

Ap Liu Street Flea Market (p127) Quirky finds like rare batteries and satellite dishes.

Stanley Market (p87) Clothes, Chinese souvenirs, lacework, even wetsuits; and food nearby.

Wan Chai's Markets (p82) Food, funerary offerings, incense and spice shops along several streets.

Best **Budget Eats & Street Food**

It is not difficult to eat well and cheaply in Hong Kong, compared to Tokyo or London. If you're looking to spend under $200 per person on a meal, there are good Chinese and South Asian options aplenty. For anything under $100, your dining room would be a noodle and congee shop, *cha chaan tang*, *dai pai dong* or fast-food chain.

Cha Chaan Tang

The quintessential Hong Kong eatery, the 'tea cafe' appeared in the 1940s to provide cheap Western-style snacks to people who couldn't afford Earl Grey and cucumber sandwiches. Most, like **Mido Cafe** (p121), serve sandwiches, noodles, and tea or coffee with milk; some also serve rice dishes, curries and seafood, and Western-inspired pastries such as egg custard tarts.

Dai Pai Dong

After WWII, the government issued licences to the families of deceased civil servants so that they could operate food stalls for a living. The licence was physically big, so locals referred to these eateries as 'big licence stall' *(dai pai dong)*. Traditionally, they are open-air hawker-style places, but many have been relocated to 'cooked-food centres' in buildings for easier management. Operators may serve anything from congee and sandwiches to hotpots and seafood.

☑ **Top Tips**

▶ To save money, go to a *cha chaan tang* for the breakfast set or tea set. Portions are slightly smaller than a la carte. All sets come with a drink.

Best Dai Pai Dong

Temple Street Night Market (p114) Both stalls and under-the-stars; quick bites and hotpots.

Ap Lei Chau Market Cooked Food Centre (p90) They'll also cook seafood bought from the market downstairs.

Lan Fong Yuen (p51) Noodles, pastries and Hong Kong–style milk tea.

Temple Street Night Market (p114)

Best Noodle and Congee Shops

Nathan Congee and Noodle (p120) Charming 50-year-old shop.

Good Hope Noodle (p120) Michelin-crowned noodle and congee place.

Tasty Congee & Noodle Wonton Shop (p37) Yummy Michelin-endorsed noodles, congee and dishes in upmarket surrounds.

Kau Kee (p38) Celebrated for its beef brisket with noodles.

Best Asian Eateries

Old Bazaar Kitchen (p75) Laudable Malaysian or Chinese-Malaysian dishes.

Ziafat (p103) Arabic and Indian, but more Indian than Arabic; and shisha.

Woodlands (p105) Popular place for Indian vegetarian food.

Best European Eateries

Linguini Fini (p38) Casual Italian in a cosy setting.

La Creperie (p75) Authentic crepes and galettes.

Life Cafe (p49) Creative vegetarian or vegan fare for dine-in or takeaway.

Best Chinese Budget Restaurants

Vbest Tea House (p50) Cantonese home-cooking and great teas.

Din Tai Fung (p104) Shanghainese and northern classics by a Taiwanese chain.

Ser Wong Fun (p51) Old-school Cantonese dishes and snake soup.

Spring Deer (p105) Solid Northern Chinese fare; very busy.

Best for Local Edibles

Honeymoon Dessert (p137) Chinese-style desserts made with fruits or pulses.

Yiu Fung Store (p83) A speciality store for traditional Chinese snacks.

Kowloon Soy Company (p57) An old shop famous for its Chinese condiments and snacks.

Best **Dim Sum**

Dim sum are tidbits consumed with tea for breakfast or lunch. The term literally means 'to touch the heart' and the act of eating dim sum – a strictly Cantonese practice – is yum cha, meaning 'to drink tea'. Each dish, often containing two to four morsels steamed in a bamboo basket, is meant to be shared.

GAVIN HELLIER/GETTY IMAGES ©

Best Overall

Luk Yu Teahouse (p49) Old-school excellence; unbeatable decor.

Ye Shanghai (p105) Cantonese and Shanghainese favourites in an elegant setting.

Tim Ho Wan (p121) Cheap and cheery, and comes with Michelin stars.

Best Budget Places

Dah Wing Wah (p137) Solid traditional selections in far-flung Yuen Long.

Tim Ho Wan (p121) There's a well-rewarded wait for their low-price dim sum.

Best Midrange Dim Sum

Luk Yu Teahouse (p49) Hong Kong's best-known teahouse.

City Hall Maxim's Palace (p38) A huge selection of dim sum in a massive dining room.

Tim's Kitchen (p36) Well executed and well loved, in a quiet part of town.

Best Luxury Tidbits

Lung King Heen (p37) Top-notch vistas and Michelin-crowned creations.

Manor Seafood Restaurant (p75) Excellent old-school fare in a famously low-key environment.

Ming Court (p120) Modern decor and delightful tidbits in Mong Kok.

Best for Ambience

Luk Yu Teahouse (p49) Eastern art-deco setting with whirling fans and stained-glass windows.

Lung King Heen (p37) A sleek and modern dining room with awesome views.

Jumbo Kingdom Floating Restaurant (p91) Memorable kitsch and harbour views, almost like a movie set.

City Hall Maxim's Palace (p38) A typical yum-cha experience in a large noisy hall.

Best
Drinking &
Nightlife

Lan Kwai Fong and Soho are the best areas for bars; they're full of life and revellers almost every night. Pubs in Wan Chai are cheaper and more relaxed, though a few sleek addresses have sprung up in the Star St neighbourhood. Watering holes in Tsim Sha Tsui tend to attract a more local clientele.

CATHERINE KARNOW/CORBIS ©

Most Stylish Decor

Sevva (p39) Sleek and tastefully dramatic.

The Pawn (p77) Old pawn shop with shabby-chic interiors.

Felix (pictured above right; p108) Designed by Philippe Starck.

Best for Meeting Nonposeurs

Club 71 (p45) Artist and activist hang-out.

Bar 42 (p52) You'll drink with journalists and entrepreneurs.

Liberty Exchange (p39) Frequented by finance-industry types.

Agave (p77) Sports players and salsa dancers.

Best for Live Music

Peel Fresco (p56) Mainly jazz.

Backstage Live Restaurant (p54) Indie bands.

Grappa's Cellar (p39) Swing, electronic, jazz.

Makumba (p44) Afro-jazz.

Best Pubs

The Globe (p52) Spacious and homey.

Delaney's (p77) Two-floor Irish pub.

Ned Kelly's Last Stand (p107) Quirky and loads of fun with a live band.

Carnegie's (p77) Known for its bar-counter dancing.

Best Whisky Bars

Macallan Whisky Bar & Lounge, Macau (p154) Arguably the best in Hong Kong and Macau.

Angel's Share (p52) Clubby place specialising in Irish whiskey.

b.a.r. Executive Bar (p77) Japanese-style bar; by appointment only.

Butler (p107) Japanese bartending excellence in Kowloon.

Best Wine Spots

Crown Wine Cellars (p90) Great bottles in a historic building.

8th Estate Winery (p89) A winery inside a factory building.

Amo Eno (p39) American-owned wine bar at the IFC.

Flying Winemaker (p45) Handcrafted bottles by a local winemaker.

Best
Fine Dining

PAMELA LAO/GETTY IMAGES ©

Those with a large pocket are spoilt for choice in Hong Kong when it comes to haute cuisine, from braised abalone and lobster sashimi to the fancy molecular creations of the latest celebrity chef. Prices at the top addresses can be steep, but the city's gourmands don't seem to mind – they're fully booked almost any night of the week.

Haute Cantonese

Hong Kong's dominant cuisine is Cantonese, the most sophisticated of China's eight regional cuisines. It's one that's known for complex cooking methods, an obsession with freshness, and the use of a wide range of ingredients. The coastal location has also meant that Cantonese kitchens enjoy access to some very costly marine life, such as deep-sea fish, and gigantic lobsters. That is why even Northern Chinese cooks would acknowledge the superiority of their Cantonese colleagues in making the best of exclusive items like abalone.

Celebrity Chefs

Hong Kong's affluent and cosmopolitan population loves foreign food, especially Japanese and European. This is evidenced by the sheer number of exclusive sushi bars you can find in town and the population of eponymous restaurants opened by international celebrity chefs such as Nobuyuki 'Nobu' Matsuhisa, Joël Robuchon and Pierre Gagnaire.

☑ **Top Tip**

▶ **Home Dining HK** (家常便飯; ☎5680 6089; homedining hk@gmail.com; $400 per person) arranges dinner (including watching preparations) at a local home. Contact them two or three weeks ahead of time.

Best Overall

Gaddi's (p104) Impeccable French food and pristine service.

Gold by Harlan Goldstein (p49) Modern Italian prepared with heart.

Sushi Kuu (p50) Fresh seafood in generous portions.

Yin Yang (p73) Chinese dishes full of pleasant surprises.

Nobu restaurant

Best for Chinese

Yin Yang (p73) Chinese with modern influences.

Manor Seafood Restaurant (p75) Old-school Cantonese, including rare dishes.

The Chairman (p36) Simple Cantonese cooked with top-notch ingredients.

Ye Shanghai (p105) Modern Shanghainese loved by locals and tourists.

Best for Seafood

Lamcombe Seafood Restaurant (p141) Great choice of venue for a seafood feast.

Manor Seafood Restaurant (p75) Steamed crab is the speciality.

Sushi Kuu (p50) Fresh fish is flown in daily from Japan.

Best for European

Gaddi's (p104) French food masterfully prepared since 1953.

Gold by Harlan Goldstein (p49) Italian dishes featuring a lot of seafood.

Cépage (p74) A modern slant on classic French.

Ammo (p70) Spanish tapas and Italian mains.

Best for Japanese

Sushi Kuu (p50) One of the best sushi bars in town.

Iroha (p67) Japanese-style grilled meat specialist with a huge range of cuts.

Irori (p75) Innovative sushi and cooked dishes with a modern twist.

Best for Ambience

Ammo (p70) Chic ammo-inspired decor in the hills of Admiralty.

Yin Yang (p73) Faux-rustic decor inside a historic building.

Ye Shanghai (p105) Elegant interiors with huge windows.

Best for Views

Lung King Heen (p37) Sweeping harbour views.

Shatin 18 (p137) Overlooking hills in Sha Tin.

Ammo (p70) Lush environs in Admiralty.

Caprice (p38) Harbour sights run the length of the room through a wall of glass.

Best
Gay & Lesbian

WOODY WU/REUTERS/CORBIS ©

While Hong Kong's gay scene may not have the vibrancy or visibility of cities like Sydney, it has made huge strides in recent years. Two decades ago, it had no more than a couple of grotty speakeasies. Today Hong Kong counts more than two dozen bars and clubs, and just as many gay-oriented saunas.

Attitude to Homosexuality

It was only in 1991 that the Crimes (Amendment) Ordinance removed criminal penalties for homosexual acts between consenting adults over the age of 18 (the criminal laws against male homosexuality were initially a product of British colonialism, with a maximum sentence of life imprisonment). Since then, gay groups have been lobbying for legislation to address the issue of discrimination on the grounds of sexual orientation, but to date there's still no law against it in Hong Kong. Neither is there legal recognition for same-sex marriages. That said, Hong Kong Chinese society is, in general, a lot more accepting of homosexuality than it was 10 years ago.

Best Bars & Clubs

T:ME (p52) A small and trendy bar off Hollywood Rd.

Volume (p52) Cocktail bar with a dance floor.

DYMK (p52) 'Does your mother know?'; an upscale bar.

Best for Shopping

DMop (p82) Edgy street fashion.

G.O.D. (p81) Lifestyle products with cheeky retro motifs.

Horizon Plaza (p93) Furniture and clothing.

☑ Top Tips

▶ For information on Hong Kong Pride Parade visit http://hkpride.

▶ **Les Peches** (9101 8001; lespeches info@yahoo.com) has monthly events for lesbians and bisexual women.

▶ **Dim Sum** (http://dimsum-hk.com) has free monthly listings.

▶ Gay-centric travel agent **OUTconcorde** (2526 3391; www .outconcorde.com; 1st fl, Galuxe Bldg, 8-10 On Lan St, Central).

▶ **Gay Home Stay HK** (5100 6877; www.gayhome stayhk.com) offers lodging.

Best
For Kids

Hong Kong is a great travel destination for kids, though the crowds, traffic and pollution might take some parents a little getting used to. Food and sanitation are of a high standard. The city is jam-packed with things to entertain the young ones, often just a hop, skip and jump away from attractions for you.

Best for Young Children

Hong Kong Space Museum (p97) Plenty of opportunities for kids to test their motor skills.

Hong Kong Science Museum (p97) Three storeys of action-packed displays, including a play area for toddlers.

Middle Road Children's Playground (p101) Swings, slides and climbing facilities.

Hong Kong Zoological & Botanical Gardens (pictured above right; p33) Flamingos, baboons, storks and tortoises.

Best for Older Kids and Preteens

Ocean Park (p89) Hong Kong's premier amusement park.

Hong Kong Science Museum (p97) Multimedia, hands-on displays spread out over three storeys.

Hong Kong Wetland Park (p134) Themed exhibits, a theatre and play facilities.

Hong Kong Heritage Museum (p134) The museum has an excellent children's discovery centre.

Best Shopping for Kids

Tai Yuen Street in Wan Chai (p82) Known for its traditional toy shops.

Ocean Terminal (p111) The ground floor has a collection of shops for kids.

Horizon Plaza (p93) Has megastores selling kids' books and clothing.

☑ Top Tips

▶ For more ideas check out this booklet from the tourism board: www.discover hongkong.com/ promotions/family/ eng/html/front/ index.html.

▶ **La Leche League Hong Kong** (www.lllhk .org) is an English-speaking breast-feeding support group.

▶ Nursing rooms are available in large malls and museums.

▶ **Rent-a-Mum** (☏ 2523 4868; www .rent-a-mum.com; $120-140/hr, min 4hr) has child-minding services (note transport charges may be added).

DANITA DELIMONT/ALAMY ©

Best
For Free

Hong Kong is not a cheap city to visit by any means, but sometimes a little imagination can help keep your pockets full. Not only that, going creatively cheap can sometimes reward you with riches the moneyed never even dream about. Here are some free (or almost free) options in Hong Kong, besides the usual suspects like parks, beaches, temples and markets.

Best History for Free

Ping Shan Heritage Trail (p135) Magnificent buildings in a walled village.

Former Marine Police Headquarters (p100) One of the oldest remaining government buildings.

Hong Kong Cemetery (p67) Reads like a 'who's who' of dead Hong Kong.

Best Culture for Free

Street Music Concert (p78) Excellent concert under the stars.

Taichi (pictured above right; p99) The Hong Kong Tourism Board treats you to a free taichi lesson.

Wan Chai's Upright Artists' Village (p70) Artists and a bookstore in an old tenement building.

Best Art for Free

Para/Site Art Space (p35) A small gallery with big ideas.

C&G Artpartment (p119) Politically minded art in Mong Kok.

Jockey Club Creative Arts Centre (p127) Artists' studios in a former factory.

Best Vibe for Free

Happy Valley Racecourse (p64) Bring wine and chestnuts, and win more than $10 to cover your admission.

LONELY PLANET/GETTY IMAGES ©

☑ **Top Tip**

▶ For a cheaper trip to the movies, visit on Tuesdays, when you can pay up to $25 less.

Chungking Mansions (p100) A global village in the heart of Tsim Sha Tsui.

Southorn Playground (p66) The social hub of old Wan Chai.

Survival Guide

Survival Guide

Before You Go

When to Go

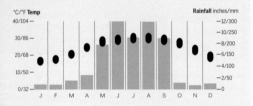

°C/°F Temp
Rainfall inches/mm

40/104 —
30/86 —
20/68 —
10/50 —
0/32 —

— 12/300
— 10/250
— 8/200
— 6/150
— 4/100
— 2/50
— 0

J F M A M J J A S O N D

➔ **Mar–May** Asia's top film festival, a rugby tournament, an art fair and deities' birthdays await in the warm and wet city.

➔ **Jun–Aug** Something hot (the beach, a new wardrobe), something wet (dragon-boat races, beer): your antidotes to sultry summers.

➔ **Sep–Nov** Head for the hills by day, enjoy an arts festival by night – autumn is the best time to visit Hong Kong.

➔ **Dec–Feb** Chilly with occasional rain, Hong Kong celebrates Chinese New Year under Christmas lights.

Book Your Stay

☑ **Top Tip** Booking a room is not essential outside peak periods, but during the shoulder and low seasons, you can get discounts of up to 50% off rack rates if you book online.

➔ If you're on a tight budget, your options on the Island side are more or less limited to busy Causeway Bay, which is great for shopping. Over the water, Tsim Sha Tsui is rammed with budget places, mostly tiny guesthouses. It's livelier, too.

➔ For those seeking a midpriced stay, Wan Chai, on Hong Kong Island, has plenty of midrange places, some at reasonable rates. Tsim Sha Tsui and Kowloon, however, offer by far the most bang for your midrange buck.

➔ If you have cash, Hong Kong is your playground. The top-end hotels here are some of the best in the world.

➜ Hong Kong's two accommodation high seasons are from March to April and October to November, though things can get tight around Chinese New Year (late January or February) as well. Rates drop outside these periods, sometimes substantially.

Useful Websites

Hong Kong Hotels Association (www.hkha.org) Offers up to 50% discount on over a hundred midrange and high-end hotels.

www.taketraveller.com Offers similar deals as the HKHA.

Country & Marine Parks Authority (☏1823; www.afcd.gov.hk) Maintains 40 campgrounds.

Hong Kong Youth Hostels Association (香港青年旅舍協會; HKYHA; ☏2788 1638; www.yha.org.hk; Shop 118, 1st fl, Fu Cheong Shopping Centre, Shum Mong Rd, Sham Shui Po; ⓂNam Cheong, exit A) Has Hostelling International (HI)–affiliated hostels.

Lonely Planet (www.lonelyplanet.com) Author-recommended reviews and online booking.

Best Budget

Helena May (www.helenamay.com) Admiralty's colonial candidate has affordable accommodation, but conditions apply.

Salisbury (www.ymcahk.org.hk) This YMCA-run hostel offers great value plus harbour views in Tsim Sha Tsui.

Hop Inn (www.hopinn.hk) Guesthouse in Tsim Sha Tsui with small but spotless rooms designed by local artists.

Y-Loft Square Youth Hostel (www.youthsquare.hk) Clean, cheerful rooms that are relatively large, in Chai Wan.

Best Midrange

Hotel LKF (www.hotel-lkf.com.hk) High-tech rooms in muted tones, in the thick of the Lan Kwai Fong action.

Harbour View (www.theharbourview.com.hk) Excellent value next to the Hong Kong Arts Centre in Wan Chai.

Madera (www.hotelmadera.com.hk) Rooms with Spanish themes in the heart of Yau Ma Tei.

Fleming (www.thefleming.com) A chic address offering homey accommodation in Wan Chai.

Best Top End

Mandarin Oriental (www.mandarinoriental.com.hk) This hotel in Central has long been considered one of the world's best.

Four Seasons (www.fourseasons.com/hongkong) Contemporary decor, harbour views and pristine service.

Landmark Oriental (www.mandarinoriental.com.hk) The Mandarin Oriental's hotel geared for business travellers.

Hyatt Regency Tsim Sha Tsui (http://hongkong.tsimshatsui.hyatt.com) A Tsim Sha Tsui classic that continues to offer superlative service.

Best for Families

InterContinental (www.intercontinental.com) Top-notch service at a prime waterfront location in Tsim Sha Tsui.

Burlington II (www.burlington-hk.com) Some 80 bright (but pricey) serviced apartments in Wan Chai.

Salisbury (www.ymcahk.org
.hk) Rooms and dormitories with harbour views in Tsim Sha Tsui.

Island Shangri-la (www
.shangri-la.com) A swish number in the eastern part of Tsim Sha Tsui.

BP International (www
.bpih.com.hk) This large hotel overlooking Kowloon Park has family rooms.

Boat Moksha (www.wimdu
.com) An affordable B&B inside a houseboat moored at Aberdeen.

Arriving in Hong Kong

☑ **Top Tip** For the best way to get to your accommodation, see p17.

Hong Kong International Airport

→ The **Airport Express** (www.mtr.com.hk) is the fastest and most expensive way to get to and from HKIA. It departs daily every 10 to 12 minutes, 6am to 1am, for Hong Kong station ($100, 24 minutes) in Central, calling at Kowloon station ($90) in Jordan and at Tsing Yi Island ($60) en route.

→ An Octopus card (p187) or Airport Express Travel Pass allows three days of unlimited travel on the MTR and Light Rail and one/two trips on the Airport Express ($220/$300).

→ If you are taking the Airport Express to the airport, most airlines allow you to check in your bags and receive your boarding pass from one day to 90 minutes before your flight at Hong Kong or Kowloon **Airport Express stations** (⊙ 5.30am-12.30am).

→ Major hotel and guesthouse areas on Hong Kong Island are served by Air Buses (every 10 to 30 minutes from 6am to midnight). For Central, Sheung Wan, Admiralty, Wan Chai and Causeway Bay take Air Bus A11 ($40); for the south take the A10 ($48); for Tsim Sha Tsui, Yau Ma Tei and Mong Kok take the A21 ($33).

→ Night buses are designated 'N'. Buy your ticket at the booth near the airport bus stand.

→ Sample taxi fares from the airport: Central, Sheung Wan, Admiralty, Wan Chai and Causeway Bay: $300; the south

$320 to $350; Tsim Sha Tsui, Yau Ma Tei and Mong Kok: $230.

Lo Wu or Lok Ma Chau

→ If you cross the border from Shenzhen via the Lo Wu or Lok Ma Chau border gates, take the MTR East Rail line after passing through customs. You can change to destinations in Kowloon at Kowloon Tong station and to destinations in Hong Kong Island at Tsim Sha Tsui station.

→ If you take cross-border buses from Guangdong to Hong Kong, you'll need to alight from and reboard the buses before and after going through customs in Lo Wu or Lok Ma Chau. Almost all buses stop near MTR stations so you can either change to MTR or taxi, depending on your destination. Check **CTS Express Coach** (http://ctsbus.hkcts.com) and **Trans-Island Limousine Service** (www.trans-island .com.hk) for departure and arrival points of cross-border buses.

Macau Ferry Terminal

➡ You can reach Hong Kong from Macau and Guangdong by frequent ferry services. Macau to Hong Kong: **Turbojet** (www.turbojet.com.hk) and **Cotai Jet** (www.cotaijet .com.mo). Guangdong to Hong Kong: **Chu Kong Passenger Transportation Company** (www.cksp .com.hk).

➡ You will arrive in Hong Kong either at the Hong Kong–Macau Ferry Terminal or the China Ferry Terminal. The former is located next to the Sheung Wan MTR station, which is stops away from destinations on Hong Kong Island. The China Ferry Terminal is a 15-minute walk from Tsim Sha Tsui MTR station.

Getting Around

In this book, the nearest metro, bus, train/tram or ferry route is noted after the 🚇, 🚌, 🚆 or 🚢 in each listing. See also the transport map on this book's pull-out map.

Travel Passes

The **Octopus card** (www.octopuscards.com) is a rechargeable 'smart card' valid on the MTR and most forms of public transport in Hong Kong. It even allows you to make purchases at retail outlets across the territory. It costs $150 ($70 for children and seniors), which includes a $50 refundable deposit and $100 worth of travel. Octopus fares are about 5% cheaper than ordinary ones on the MTR. You can buy a card and recharge at any MTR station.

For shorter stays there's the new **MTR Tourist Day Pass** ($55), valid on the MTR for 24 hours after the first use.

Bus

☑ **Best for**... rural destinations without any MTR stations nearby.

➡ Hong Kong's extensive bus system runs from 5.30 or 6am to midnight or 12.30am, with night-bus service from 12.45am to 5am, and goes just about everywhere in the territory. You will need exact change or an Octopus card (p187).

➡ Central's most important terminal for buses is below Exchange Square (Map p30, F3). In Kowloon the Star Ferry bus terminal (Map p98, B4) has buses heading up Nathan Rd and to the Hung Hom train station.

➡ **City Bus** and **New World First Bus** (www .nwstbus.com.hk) and

Kowloon Motor Bus (www.kmb.hk) provide user-friendly route searching on their websites.

Ferry

☑ **Best for**... crossing Victoria Harbour from Central to Tsim Sha Tsui or vice versa.

➡ There are two Star Ferry routes. The more popular is the one running between Central (Outlying Islands ferry terminal, pier 7; Map p30, G1) and Tsim Sha Tsui (Map p98, B4). Fares are $2/3 (lower/upper deck). The Star Ferry also links Wan Chai with Tsim Sha Tsui. For more on the Star Ferry, see p26.

➡ Two separate ferry companies operate services to the outlying islands, including Lantau, Cheung Chau and Lamma, from ferry terminal piers 4, 5 and 6 (Map p30, F1) in Central: **New World First Ferry Services Ltd** (www.nwff .com.hk) and **Hong Kong & Kowloon Ferry Ltd** (www.hkkf.com.hk).

Metro

☑ **Best for**... most urban destinations.

➡ The **Mass Transit Railway** (MTR; ☎ 2881 8888; www.mtr.com.hk; fares $4-25; ⏰ 6am-midnight or 1am) has 10 lines, including the Airport Express line (p186). Ticket machines accept notes and coins and dispense change.

➡ The longer-distance MTR East Rail line, which runs from Hung Hom station to Lo Wu or Lok Ma Chau on the mainland border, and the West Rail line, which links East Tsim Sha Tsui station with Tuen Mun in the New Territories, offer the fastest route to the New Territories.

Minibus

☑ **Best for**... rural destinations without any MTR stations nearby.

➡ Also known as 'public light buses', minibuses seat up to 16 people. Small red 'minibuses' ($2 to $22) don't run regular routes; you can get on or off by request unless restricted by road rules. Green 'maxicabs' make designated stops.

Taxi

☑ **Best for**... late hours when the MTR has stopped running and traffic is light.

➡ Hong Kong taxis are a bargain compared to taxis in other world-class cities. Some sample fares:

Route	Fare
Central MTR station to Causeway Bay	$40
Central MTR station to Victoria Peak	$50
Central MTR station to Tsim Sha Tsui	$80
Tsim Sha Tsui to Sai Kung	$120
Tung Chung to Tian Tan Buddha	$145

Tram

☑ **Best for**... sightseeing and when you're not in a hurry.

➡ For a flat fare of $2.50 (dropped in a box beside the driver as you disembark) you can rattle along on Hong Kong Island's double-decker **tram** (www .hktramways.com; ⏰ 6am-12.30am) as far as you like, over 16km of track.

➡ There are six routes but they all move on the same tracks along the northern coast of Hong Kong Island. The longest run (Kennedy Town–Shau Kei Wan, with a change at Western Market) takes about 1½ hours. For more tram information, see p76.

Essential Information

Business Hours

☑ **Top Tip** Banks and post offices are closed on Sundays.

Exceptions to the following hours are noted in listings.

Restaurants Smaller eateries from 7am or 8am to 11pm; formal restaurants from 11am to at least 10pm

Shops 10am or 11am to 9pm or 10pm

Customs Regulations

➡ The duty-free allowance for visitors arriving in Hong Kong (including those coming from Macau and mainland China) is 19 cigarettes (or 1 cigar or 25g of tobacco) and 1L of spirits. Apart from these limits there are few other import taxes.

Electricity

220V/50Hz

Emergencies

Police, Fire & Ambulance (☎999)

Practicalities

Metric System The metric system is officially used, but traditional Chinese weights and measures persist at local markets, including *leung* (37.8g) and *gan* (catty; about 605g). There are 16 *leung* to the *gan*.

Newspapers & Magazines The local English-language newspapers are the *South China Morning Post* (www.scmp.com), published daily ($7), and the *Standard* (www.thestandard.com.hk), published Monday to Saturday ($6). The Beijing mouthpiece *China Daily* (www.chinadaily.com.cn) prints a Hong Kong English-language edition ($6).

Radio Popular English-language stations in Hong Kong are RTHK Radio 3 (current affairs and talk radio; 567AM, 1584AM, 97.9FM and 106.8FM), RTHK Radio 4 (classical music; 97.6FM–98.9FM), RTHK Radio 6 (BBC World Service relays; 675AM), AM 864 (hit parade; 864AM) and Metro Plus (news; 1044AM).

Time Hong Kong Standard Time is eight hours ahead of GMT; there is no daylight saving time in summer.

TV The two English-language terrestrial stations are TVB Pearl and ATV World.

Internet Access

Wi-fi is widely available. A 60-minute PCCW Wi-fi pass is available at HKTB visitor centres.

Free wi-fi can be found at:

➡ Parks, public libraries, sports centres,

museums, cooked-food markets, community halls, and government premises (see www.gov.hk/en/theme/wifi/location)

➡ Hong Kong International Airport

➡ McDonald's (www.mcdonalds.com.hk), Pacific

Dos & Don'ts

There aren't many unusual rules of etiquette to follow in Hong Kong; in general, common sense will take you as far as you'll need to go. But on matters of identity, appearance and gift-giving, local people might see things a little differently from you.

Clothing

Beyond the suited realm of business, smart-casual dress is acceptable even at swish restaurants. On the beach, topless is a local turn-off and nudity a definite no-no.

Colours

Some colours hold different symbolic meaning in Chinese culture compared to Western cultures. Red means happiness, good luck and health (though writing in red can convey anger or unfriendliness). White symbolises death, so avoid giving white flowers (except at funerals).

Dining

Dining in Hong Kong is an all-in affair: everyone shares dishes and chats loudly. Wait for others to start before digging in; if you can't manage chopsticks, don't be afraid to ask for a fork (most Chinese restaurants have them). Don't stick chopsticks upright into a bowl of rice as they can look like incense sticks in a bowl of ashes (an offering to the dead). When someone pours you tea, tap the table lightly with your index and middle finger, rather than try to mutter 'thanks' with a mouth full of food. Cover your mouth with your hand when using a toothpick.

Gifts

If you want to give flowers, chocolates or wine to someone (a fine idea if invited to their home), they may appear reluctant to accept for fear of seeming greedy, but insist and they'll give in and take them.

Coffee (www.pacificcoffee.com) and Starbucks (www.starbucks.com.hk) outlets (with purchase)

A 3G rechargeable SIM card (from $48) will connect your phone to the internet at reasonable rates. Available at PCCW and SmarTone shops.

PCCW provides close to 10,000 hotspots where you can access wi-fi. Check service plans at www.pccwwifi.com/eng.

Money
Local currency

➜ One Hong Kong dollar (HK$) equals 100 cents. (One Macau pataca, or MOP, equals 100 cents and comes in the same denominations.)

➜ **Notes** $10, $20, $50, $100, $500 and $1000.

➜ **Coins** 10¢, 20¢, 50¢, $1, $2, $5 and $10.

➜ **ATMs** widely available; international travellers can withdraw funds from home accounts.

Credit cards

Visa, MasterCard, American Express, Diners Club and JCB are widely accepted. For 24-hour card cancellations or assistance, try the following numbers:

American Express (📞2811 6122)

Diners Club (📞2860 1888)

MasterCard (📞800 966 677)

Visa (📞800 900 782)

Tipping

➡ Hong Kong is not a particularly tip-conscious place; taxi drivers only expect you to round up to the nearest dollar.

➡ Tip hotel staff $10 to $20, and if you make use of the porters at the airport, $2 to $5 a suitcase is expected.

➡ Most hotels and many restaurants add a 10% service charge to the bill (see boxed text, p47).

Organised Tours

Hong Kong Tourism Board (HKTB; 📞2508 1234; www.discoverhongkong .com) runs some of the best tours; tours run by individual companies can usually be booked at any HKTB branch (see p192).

Secret Hong Kong Tour (www.secrettourhk.com) organises tours to less touristy parts of the territory.

Hong Kong Dolphinwatch (📞2984 1414; www.hkdolphinwatch.com) offers four-hour dolphin-spotting expeditions departing at 8.50am from Kowloon Hotel in Tsim Sha Tsui every Wednesday, Friday and Sunday.

Star Ferry Harbour Tour (📞2118 6201; www.starferry .com.hk/tour) is the easiest way to see the full extent of Victoria Harbour from sea level; most depart from the Star Ferry Pier in Tsim Sha Tsui (Map p98, B4).

Kayak & Hike (📞9300 5197; www.kayak-and-hike .com) takes you in a junk to a kayak base near Bluff Island, from where you will paddle to a beach to enjoy swimming and snorkelling. Departs at 8.45am from Sai Kung old pier ($700, seven hours).

Sky Bird Travel (📞2736 2282; www.skybird.com.hk) will teach you about taichi, feng shui and Chinese tea on a four-hour tour ($298), departing at 7.30am from the Excelsior Hong Kong Hotel in Causeway Bay and at 7.45am from the Salisbury YMCA in Tsim Sha Tsui every Monday, Wednesday and Friday.

Public Holidays

New Year's Day 1 January

Chinese New Year 11 to 13 February 2013, 31 January to 2 February 2014

Easter 29 March to 1 April 2013, 18 to 21 April 2014

Ching Ming 4 April

Money-Saving Tips

➡ Take the super-efficient MTR and only change to taxi if needed. See the boxed text Travel Passes, p187.

➡ Head to museums on Wednesdays when they have free entry, and visit night markets (also free). See p182 for more ideas on free stuff.

Labour Day 1 May

Buddha's Birthday 17 May 2013, 6 May 2014

Dragon Boat (Tuen Ng) Festival 12 June 2013, 2 June 2014

Hong Kong SAR Establishment Day 1 July

Mid-Autumn Festival 20 September 2013, 9 September 2014

China National Day 1 October

Chung Yeung 14 October 2013, 2 October 2014

Christmas Day 25 December

Boxing Day 26 December

Telephone

➔ Mobile phones work everywhere – even in tunnels and the MTR. Any GSM-compatible phone can be used in Hong Kong.

➔ **PCCW** (☑2888 2888; www.pccw.com) has retail outlets throughout the territory, where you can buy phonecards, mobile phones and accessories. Handsets can be rented from $35 per day. A SIM card with prepaid call time can be as cheap as $50.

➔ Phonecards are available at 7-Eleven and Circle K stores.

Useful Phone Numbers

Country code ☑852 (☑853 for Macau)

International dialling code ☑001

International directory enquiries ☑10015

Local directory enquiries ☑1081

Reverse-charge/collect calls ☑10010

Time & temperature ☑18501

Weather ☑187 8200

Tourist Information

➔ The very efficient and friendly **Hong Kong Tourism Board** (HKTB; www.discoverhongkong.com) produces reams of useful pamphlets and publications. Its website is also a good point of reference.

➔ There are HKTB branches at **Hong Kong International Airport** (⊙7am-11pm), the **Star Ferry Concourse** (Map p98, B4; ⊙8am-8pm) in Tsim Sha Tsui and the **Peak Piazza** (⊙9am-9pm) at Victoria Peak. Alter-natively, call the **HKTB Visitor Hotline** (☑2508 1234; ⊙9am-6pm) if you have a query or problem or if you're lost; you'll find staff eager to help.

Travellers with Disabilities

➔ Disabled people will have to cope with MTR stairs as well as pedestrian overpasses, narrow footpaths and steep hills. People whose sight or hearing is impaired must be cautious of Hong Kong's demon drivers. On the other hand, some stairs in MTR stations and most buses are now accessible by wheelchair, taxis are never hard to find, and most buildings have lifts (many with Braille panels). Wheelchairs can negotiate the lower decks of most of the ferries, and almost all public toilets now have access for the disabled.

➔ **Hong Kong Society for Rehabilitation** (香港復康會; ☑3143 2800; www.accessguide.hk) has a website that offers practical information for travellers with disabilities.

Language

Cantonese is the most popular Chinese dialect in Hong Kong. Cantonese speakers can read Chinese characters, but will pronounce many characters differently from a Mandarin speaker.

Cantonese has 'tonal' quality – the raising and lowering of pitch on certain syllables. Tones fall on vowels and on the consonant **n**. Our pronunciation guides show five tones, indicated by accent marks – **à** (high), **á** (high rising), **à** (low falling), **á** (low rising), **a** (low) – plus a level tone (**a**).

To enhance your trip with a phrasebook, visit **lonelyplanet.com**. Lonely Planet iPhone phrasebooks are available through the Apple App store.

Basics

Hello.	哈佬。	hàa·ló
Goodbye.	再見。	joy·gin
How are you?	你幾好啊嗎?	láy gáy hó à maa
Fine.	幾好。	gáy hó
Please ...	唔該……	ǹg·gòy ...
Thank you.	多謝。	dàw·je
Excuse me.	對唔住。	deui·ǹg·jew
Sorry.	對唔住。	deui·ǹg·jew
Yes.	係。	hai
No.	不係。	ǹg·hai

Do you speak English?
你識唔識講英文啊? — láy sìk·ǹg·sìk gáwng yìng·mán aa

I don't understand.
我唔明。 — ngáw ǹg mìng

Eating & Drinking

I'd like..., please.
唔該我要…… — ǹg·gòy ngáw yiu ...

a table for two	兩位 嘅檯	léung wái ge tóy
the drink list	酒料單	jáu·liú·dàan
the menu	菜單	choy·dàan
beer	啤酒	bè·jáu
coffee	咖啡	gaa·fè

I don't eat ...
我唔吃…… — ngáw ǹg sik ...

fish	魚	yéw
poultry	雞鴨鵝	gài ngaap ngàw
red meat	牛羊肉	ngàu yèung yuk

Cheers!
乾杯! — gàwn·buì

That was delicious.
真好味。 — jàn hó·may

I'd like the bill, please.
唔該我要埋單。 — ǹg·gòy ngáw yiu màai·dàan

Shopping

I'd like to buy ...
我想買…… — ngáw séung máai ...

I'm just looking.
睇下。 — tái haa

How much is it?
幾多錢? — gáy·dàw chín

That's too expensive.
太貴啦。　　　　taai gwai laa

Can you lower the price?
可唔可以平　　　háw·ng·háw·yí pèng
啲呀？　　　　　dì aa

Emergencies

Help! 救命！　　gau·meng

Go away! 走開！　　jáu·hòy

Call a doctor!
快啲叫醫生！　faai·dì giu yì·sàng

Call the police!
快啲叫警察！　faai·dì giu gíng·chaat

I'm lost.
我蕩失路。　　ngáw dawng·sàk·lo

I'm sick.
我病咗。　　　ngáw beng·jáw

Where are the toilets?
廁所喺邊度？　chi·sáw hái bìn·do

Time & Numbers

What time is it?
而家　　　　　yi·gàa
幾點鐘？　　　gáy·dím·jùng

It's (10) o'clock.
(十)點鐘。　　(sap)·dím·jùng

Half past (10).
(十)點半。　　(sap)·dím bun

morning	朝早	jiù·jó
afternoon	下晝	haa·jau
evening	夜晚	ye·máan
yesterday	寢日	kàm·yat
today	今日	gàm·yat
tomorrow	听日	tìng·yat

1	一	yàt
2	二	yi
3	三	sàam
4	四	say
5	五	ńg
6	六	luk
7	七	chàt
8	八	baat
9	九	gáu
10	十	sap

Transport & Directions

Where's ...?
……喺邊度？　... hái bìn·do

What's the address?
地址係？　　　day·jí hai

How do I get there?
點樣去？　　　dím·yéung heui

How far is it?
有幾遠？　　　yáu gáy yéwn

Can you show me (on the map)?
你可唔可以　　láy háw·ng·háw·yí
(喺地圖度)指俾　(hái day·to do) jí báy
我睇我喺邊度？　ngáw tái ngáw hái bìn·do

When's the next bus?
下一班巴士　　haa·yàt·bàan bàa·sí
幾點開？　　　gáy dím hòy

A ticket to ...
一張去……　　yàt jèung heui ...
嘅飛　　　　　ge fày

Does it stop at ...?
會唔會喺　　　wuí·ng·wuí hái
……停呀？　　 ... tìng aa

I'd like to get off at ...
我要喺……　　ngáw yiu hái ...
落車　　　　　lawk·chè

Index

See also separate subindexes for:

⊗ **Eating p203**

☮ **Drinking p204**

✿ **Entertainment p205**

🔒 **Shopping p205**

Sights p000
Map Pages **p000**

Sights p000
Map Pages **p000**

Eating

Behind the Scenes

Send Us Your Feedback

We love to hear from travellers – your comments help make our books better. We read every word, and we guarantee that your feedback goes straight to the authors. Visit **lonelyplanet.com/contact** to submit your updates and suggestions.

Note: We may edit, reproduce and incorporate your comments in Lonely Planet products such as guidebooks, websites and digital products, so let us know if you don't want your comments reproduced or your name acknowledged. For a copy of our privacy policy visit lonelyplanet.com/privacy.

Our Readers

Many thanks to the travellers who used the last edition and wrote to us with helpful hints, useful advice and interesting anecdotes: Pippa Curtis, Marcus Durst, Antoine Noémie, Molly Roberts, Doris Schneidtinger, Bertrand Thierry, Joyce Van Den Oever, Laura Wong, Christopher Yang.

Piera's Thanks

I extend my warmest thanks to Venessa Cheah, Antonio Conceição Junior, Janine Cheung and Yuen Ching-sum for their knowledge and generosity. Thanks also to Carmen Ng and Catherine Fung for moral support. And to my husband Sze Pang-cheung, love and gratitude for his patience, understanding and assistance.

Acknowledgments

Cover photograph: Victoria Harbour, Hong Kong Island; TowPix/4 Corners ©

This Book

This 4th edition of Lonely Planet's *Pocket Hong Kong* was researched and written by Piera Chen. The previous edition, *Hong Kong Encounter*, was written by Piera Chen with Andrew Stone. This guidebook was commissioned in Lonely Planet's Oakland office, and produced by the following:
Commissioning Editors Emily K Wolman, Kathleen Munnelly **Coordinating Editors** Carolyn Bain, Fionn Twomey **Coordinating Cartographer** James Leversha **Coordinating Layout Designer** Clara Monitto **Managing Editors** Sasha Baskett, Brigitte Ellemor **Senior Editors** Andi Jones, Catherine Naghten **Managing Cartographers** Anita Banh, Diana von Holdt **Managing Layout Designer** Jane Hart **Assisting Editors** Andrew Bain, Ali Lemer **Cover Research** Naomi Parker **Internal Image Research** Nicholas Colicchia, Rebecca Skinner **Language Content** Branislava Vladisavljevic **Thanks to** Lucy Birchley, Janine Eberle, Ryan Evans, Ming Yan Leung, Anna Metcalfe, Sunny Or, Trent Paton, Raphael Richards, Averil Robertson, Laura Stansfeld, Gerard Walker, Juan Winata

Our Writer

Piera Chen

Born to a Shanghainese father and a Pekingnese mother in Hong Kong, Piera is a writer, editor and translator who divides her time between Hong Kong, Beijing, Vancouver and various exotic holiday destinations, real and imagined. She is a lifetime Hong Konger, an avid traveller, a devoted mother and a passionate collector of life experiences. Piera has worked on the previous edition of this book, and Lonely Planet's *Hong Kong* and *China* guides. While researching for this edition, one of her greatest joys was constantly challenging herself to see familiar landscapes with borrowed eyes. Read more about Piera at www.lonelyplanet.com/members/PieraChen.

Published by Lonely Planet Publications Pty Ltd
ABN 36 005 607 983
4th edition – Mar 2013
ISBN 978 1 74220 140 5
© Lonely Planet 2013 Photographs © as indicated 2013
10 9 8 7 6 5 4 3 2 1
Printed in China